AI-Based Metaheuristics for Information Security and Digital Media

This book examines the latest developments in Artificial Intelligence (AI)-based metaheuristics algorithms with applications in information security for digital media. It highlights the importance of several security parameters, their analysis, and validations for different practical applications. Drawing on multidisciplinary research including computer vision, machine learning, artificial intelligence, and modified/newly developed metaheuristics algorithms, it will enhance information security for society. It includes state-of-the-art research with illustrations and exercises throughout.

Advances in Metaheuristics

Series Editors: Patrick Siarry, Universite Paris-Est Creteil, France
Anand J. Kulkarni, Institute of Artificial Intelligence, MIT World Peace University, Pune, India

Handbook of AI-based Metaheuristics
Edited by Patrick Siarry and Anand J. Kulkarni

Metaheuristic Algorithms in Industry 4.0
Edited by Pritesh Shah, Ravi Sekhar, Anand J. Kulkarni, and Patrick Siarry

Constraint Handling in Cohort Intelligence Algorithm
Ishaan R. Kale and Anand J. Kulkarni

Hybrid Genetic Optimization for IC Chip Thermal Control: with MATLAB® applications
Mathew V K and Tapano Kumar Hotta

Handbook of Moth-Flame Optimization Algorithm: Variants, Hybrids, Improvements, and Applications
Edited by Seyedali Mirjalili

Combinatorial Optimization Under Uncertainty: Real-life Scenarios in Allocation Problems
Edited by Ritu Arora, Prof. Shalini Arora, Anand J. Kulkarni, and Patrick Siarry

AI-Based Metaheuristics for Information Security and Digital Media
Edited by Apoorva S. Shastri, Mangal Singh, Anand J. Kulkarni, and Patrick Siarry

For more information about this series please visit: https://www.routledge.com/Advances-in-Metaheuristics/book-series/AIM

AI-Based Metaheuristics for Information Security and Digital Media

Edited by
Dr Apoorva S. Shastri
Dr Mangal Singh
Dr Anand J. Kulkarni
Dr Patrick Siarry

CRC Press
Taylor & Francis Group
Boca Raton London New York

CRC Press is an imprint of the
Taylor & Francis Group, an **informa** business

A CHAPMAN & HALL BOOK

Designed image: Shutterstock Images

First edition published 2024
by CRC Press
6000 Broken Sound Parkway NW, Suite 300, Boca Raton, FL 33487-2742

and by CRC Press
4 Park Square, Milton Park, Abingdon, Oxon, OX14 4RN

CRC Press is an imprint of Taylor & Francis Group, LLC

Library of Congress Cataloging-in-Publication Data
Names: Shastri, Apoorva S., editor. | Singh, Mangal, editor. |
Kulkarni, Anand Jayant, editor. | Siarry, Patrick, editor.
Title: AI metaheuristics for information security in digital media /
edited by Prof. Apoorva S Shastri, Dr. Mangal Singh, Dr. Anand J Kulkarni, Dr. Patrick Siarry.
Description: First edition. | Boca Raton, FL : Chapman & Hall/CRC Press, 2023. |
Series: Advances in metaheuristics series |
Includes bibliographical references and index. |
Identifiers: LCCN 2022061375 (print) | LCCN 2022061376 (ebook) |
ISBN 9780367615420 (hbk) | ISBN 9781032524559 (pbk) | ISBN 9781003107767 (ebk)
Subjects: LCSH: Disinformation–Prevention–Data processing. |
Fake news–Prevention–Data processing. | Digital media–Security measures–Data processing. |
Metaheuristics. | Deep learning. | Artificial intelligence. | Social media and journalism. |
Journalism–Objectivity.
Classification: LCC HM1231 .A49 2023 (print) | LCC HM1231 (ebook) |
DDC 302.23/1–dc23/eng/20230130
LC record available at https://lccn.loc.gov/2022061375
LC ebook record available at https://lccn.loc.gov/2022061376

ISBN: 978-0-367-61542-0 (hbk)
ISBN: 978-1-032-52455-9 (pbk)
ISBN: 978-1-003-10776-7 (ebk)

DOI: 10.1201/9781003107767

Typeset in Sabon
by codeMantra

Contents

Preface   vii
About the Editors   xi
Contributors   xiii

1 Use of artificial intelligence and blockchain technologies
   in detecting and curbing fake news in journalism   1
   SUCHITRA PATNAIK AND SANTOSH KUMAR BISWAL

2 Blockchain technology-based fake news detection:
   Applications and future research directions   19
   SUSHEEL YADAV, OM JEE GUPTA, SUSHIL KUMAR GUPTA, AND HARISH BABU

3 Deep learning-based intelligent systems for audio abuse
   prediction: A survey   35
   KAUSTUBH V. SAKHARE AND RADHIKA V. KULKARNI

4 A comprehensive review of toxicity analysis using deep
   learning techniques   49
   PRANAV KULKARNI AND ISHAN G. GALA

5 Literature review on zero-knowledge proof and its
   applications   59
   PRIYA A. SIRSAT AND AAYUSH P. KHANDEKAR

6 Machine learning-based algorithmic comparison for
   fake news identification   67
   ANURADHA YENKIKAR, KAVITA SULTANPURE, AND MANISH BALI

7 A comprehensive review of classical and deep learning-
   based time series models   85
   ISHAN G. GALA AND PRANAV KULKARNI

8 Use of technologies in media and communication:
   Interventions of artificial intelligence in mitigating fake
   news on social media   95
   SANTOSH KUMAR BISWAL, AMBIKA SANKAR MISHRA, AND NARSINGH MAJHI

9 Robust color image watermarking using IWT and
   ensemble model with PCA-based statistical feature
   reduction   113
   SUSHMA JAISWAL AND MANOJ KUMAR PANDEY

   Index   133

Preface

With the advancement of information technology, the business world is completely transformed. It has a great impact on journalism, education, entertainment, public relations, etc. Currently, researchers and security experts have been working toward protection of significant information from attackers/hackers. However, due to different potential entry points in the network, it becomes a challenge for the security experts to remove all the vulnerabilities. Thus, the aim of this book is to give insight into the theoretical and practical development in the direction of information security. It also aims to provide a collection of state-of-the-art scientific and technical contributions in the area of artificial intelligence (AI)–based metaheuristic algorithms, dealing with machine learning (ML), deep learning (DL), cryptography, steganography, etc. and their combinations to improve information security in digital media. The detailed analysis of the research contributions in terms of processing time, security parameters, compression ratio, cyberattacks, cryptanalysis/steganalysis as well as highlighting intelligent, optimized, and practical approaches will be at the heart of the contributions. The book could be useful for scientists, professors, students as well as practitioners working in information security and digital media. The individual contributions are discussed below.

Chapter 1, 'Use of Artificial Intelligence and Blockchain Technologies in Detecting and Curbing Fake News in Journalism', is grappling with fake news, which has further repercussions on the ecology of newsroom management and society in general. With the upsurge of false information, the distrust and loss of credibility in mainstream media is on the rise. The fusion of journalism and technology has always created newer dimensions for the media industry. Out of certain solutions to combat fake news, technological interventions have been significant in this context by offering distributed, transparent networks of highly credible media platform that ascertains the veracity of online news contents. This chapter entails a discussion on the potential solutions offered by AI and blockchain technologies to curb the onslaught of disinformation and fake news.

Chapter 2, 'Blockchain Technology-Based Fake News Detection: Applications and Future Research Directions', investigates the use of blockchain technology in the fight against fake news. To do so, the characteristics of blockchain technology have been explained, and then the difficulties of blockchain technology has been discussed. In addition, a number of suggestions are provided as a roadmap for future researchers on topics that will need to be addressed in order to combat the spread of fake news. The blockchain technology is a new form of disruptive technology that has captured the interest of a significant number of researchers due to the exceptional security characteristics it possesses and the transparency it offers. Blockchain technology ensures the provenance, authenticity, and traceability of data by producing a record of transactions that is open to inspection, cannot be altered, and can be independently verified.

Chapter 3, 'Deep Learning-Based Intelligent Systems for Audio Abuse Prediction: A Survey', reviews the importance of AI-based metaheuristics for information security and digital media. Deep learning–based intelligent systems have been incredibly effective in spotting online abuses, whether they take the shape of text-based tweets, videos, or even memes that are just pictures or images. However, there is less attention by the research community toward automated prediction of audio abuse. This chapter focuses on the challenging task of audio abuse prediction. It presents a survey on conventional audio processing–based detection system, and different DL approaches for recognizing abusive/hate speech in audio. These approaches incorporate transfer learning, emotion encoding, natural language processing, and multimodal learning.

Chapter 4, 'A Comprehensive Review of Toxicity Analysis Using Deep Learning Techniques', highlights the different DL methods for analysis of toxicity. With the world today relying more and more on digital media for daily communication, it is imperative to devise various methodologies for the analysis and the parsing of content uploaded to various media, to ensure that unsafe and inappropriate content can be removed quickly and with robustness. The need to filter out offensive language and safeguard internet users from being the targets of online abuse and cyberbullying is urgent. This manuscript focuses on the toxicity analysis and categorizing text corpora according to the subtypes of toxicity. Along with one Recurrent Neural Network model, namely Bidirectional LSTM, four models based on transformer architecture are adopted, viz. BERT, DistilBERT, RoBERTa, and ALBERT. Using the most prominent and highly influential features out of all, the comparative analysis of the models is presented.

Chapter 5, 'Literature Review on Zero-Knowledge Proof and Its Applications', presents importance of privacy techniques like zero-knowledge proofs (ZKP), since their study and development are the major areas of interest. A cryptographic method called ZKP can conceal information while still enabling data validation. In this work, we outline various schemes highlighting the value of zero-knowledge evidence in the context of cyber security and how it can reduce the risk of cyberattacks. We have discussed two models of ZKP, which are interactive and non-interactive ZKP with their applications and issues. The goal of this research is to develop communication- and computation-efficient protocols for zero-knowledge arguments and proofs of propositions that include a significant number of 'simple' predicates. The study finishes with real-world examples, practicality, and usability of zero-knowledge proof applications using blockchain, zk-SNARKs, zk-STARKs, and the cryptocurrency Zcash.

Chapter 6, 'Machine Learning-Based Algorithmic Comparison for Fake News Identification', evaluates a need to develop a system that allows users to determine whether a content is real or fake. ML classifiers have been used by researchers; however, most existing algorithms are supervised, requiring a significant amount of time and effort. Also, they mainly focus on controversial topics and tend to expose a distinctive type of news favoring certain news agencies. The impact of spreading fake news is widespread, affecting everything from formation of prejudiced opinions to changing election results in favor of certain leaders. In this chapter, we conduct a comprehensive algorithmic comparison of six ML algorithms and contrast it with other models. From results, it is observed that decision tree algorithm with 99% accuracy outperforms all other ML algorithms in Intra-model comparison. In inter-model comparison, the algorithm outperforms validated existing state-of-the-art models by ten points over the next best model.

Chapter 7, 'A Comprehensive Review of Classical and Deep Learning-Based Time Series Models', addresses the details of various time series models relevant to classical and DL based on information security and digital media. In today's finance-driven world, forecasting future results based on previous data and trends is very important to make important decisions. The stock market is one of the most prominent applications of forecasting algorithms in which the future price of the stocks can be predicted based on the previous close price of the stock. The manuscript focuses on a comprehensive review of eight different time series models, viz. AR, ARIMA, SARIMA, ARMA, SES, HWES, Prophet, and LSTM. Models are trained on stock price data, and a comparative analysis of the models is presented.

Chapter 8, 'Use of Technologies in Media and Communication: Interventions of Artificial Intelligence in Mitigating Fake News on Social Media', addresses the need for AI-based metaheuristics for social media. Social media powered by new communication technologies has grown by leaps and bounds over the years. This new form of digital social communication has been the order of the day. The digital media outlets have gained the growing acceptance among the users and still counting. However, social media is grappling with the issue of fake news which needs to be amicably addressed. Feelings or opinions instead of facts are ruling the platforms. The repercussions of fake news are increasingly apparent and drawing the attention of several quarters of the society. In this context, technological intervention is the need of the hour. The use of AI in curbing the perils of fake news is of great importance. Again, AI tools have their own advantages and shortcomings. The current chapter attempts to understand the importance of social media in the discourse of digital communication and the incorporation of AI tools in checking the ill-effects of fake news on social media platforms.

Chapter 9, 'Robust Color Image Watermarking Using IWT and Ensemble Model with PCA-Based Statistical Feature Reduction', presents a novel blind robust color image watermarking scheme using Integer wavelet transform, Bagging, and random subspace-KNN (RS-KNN) methods. Principal component analysis (PCA) reduces the number of features so that the training time can be reduced. The extraction of a watermark is considered here as a binary (0 or 1) classification problem. A binary watermark is implanted using some quantization approach. The suggested research is motivated by the excellent learning rate of the ensemble approach, which includes Bagging and the RS-KNN ML method. Two different forms of watermarks, namely signature watermarks (the original watermark) and reference watermarks (produced at random), are utilized for embedding in the suggested research. Features are extracted from the colored watermarked image to form training and testing sets. A thorough investigation has been conducted and provided both with and without PCA. The suggested watermarking method is examined in comparison to other machine learning–based image watermarking techniques and found to be durable against the majority of image attacks.

About the Editors

Dr Apoorva S. Shastri is a Research Assistant Professor at the Institute of Artificial Intelligence at the MITWPU, Pune, India. Her research interests include optimization algorithms, VLSI design, multiobjective optimization, continuous, discrete and combinatorial optimization, complex systems, and manufacturing and self-organizing systems. She has developed socio-inspired optimization methodologies such as Multi-Cohort Intelligence (Multi-CI) Algorithm, Expectation Algorithm, and Leader Advocate Believer (LAB) Algorithm.

Dr Mangal Singh is an Associate Professor at Symbiosis Institute of Technology, Symbiosis International (Deemed University). His main research interests are the development and application of optimization heuristics algorithms and their applications to various engineering fields. He is also working on signal processing for 6G and beyond wireless communication.

Dr Anand J. Kulkarni is working as a Professor and Associate Director of the Institute of Artificial Intelligence at the MITWPU, Pune, India. His research interests include optimization algorithms, multiobjective optimization, continuous, discrete and combinatorial optimization, swarm optimization, and self-organizing systems.

Dr Patrick Siarry is a Professor in Automatics and Informatics. His main research interests are the development of new stochastic global optimization heuristics and their applications to various engineering fields. He is also interested in the fitting of process models to experimental data, the learning of fuzzy rule bases and of neural networks.

Contributors

Harish Babu
Department of Mechanical
    Engineering
Indian Institute of Technology
    (Banaras Hindu University)
Varanasi, India

Manish Bali
Presidency University
Bangalore, India

Santosh Kumar Biswal
Department of Journalism and
    Mass Communication
Rama Devi Women's University
Bhubaneswar, India

Ishan G. Gala
Marathwada Mitramandal's
    College of Engineering
Pune, India

Om Jee Gupta
School of Management (PG)
Dr Vishwanath Karad MIT World
    Peace University
Pune, India

Sushil Kumar Gupta
School of Management (UG)
Dr Vishwanath Karad MIT World
    Peace University
Pune, India

Sushma Jaiswal
Department of CSIT
Guru Ghasidas Central University
Bilaspur, India

Aayush P. Khandekar
Vishwakarma Institute of
    Technology
Pune, India

Pranav Kulkarni
Marathwada Mitramandal's
    College of Engineering
Pune, India

Radhika V. Kulkarni
Pune Institute of Computer
    Technology
Pune, India

Narsingh Majhi
Department of Journalism and
    Mass Communication
Rama Devi Women's University
Bhubaneswar, India

Ambika Sankar Mishra
Department of Journalism and
    Mass Communication
Rama Devi Women's University
Bhubaneswar, India

Manoj Kumar Pandey
Department of CSIT
Guru Ghasidas Central University
Bilaspur, India

Suchitra Patnaik
Department of Communication,
School of Interdisciplinary
Studies
The English and Foreign Languages
University (Central University)
Hyderabad, India

Kaustubh V. Sakhare
Lear Corporation
Pune, India

Priya A. Sirsat
All India Shri Shivaji Memorial
Society's Institute of Information
Technology
Pune, India

Kavita Sultanpure
Pune Institute of Computer
Technology
Pune, India

Susheel Yadav
Jindal Global Business School
O.P. Jindal Global University
Sonipat, Haryana, India

Anuradha Yenkikar
Pune Institute of Computer
Technology
Pune, India

Chapter 1

Use of artificial intelligence and blockchain technologies in detecting and curbing fake news in journalism

Suchitra Patnaik

The English and Foreign Languages University (Central University)

Santosh Kumar Biswal

Rama Devi Women's University

CONTENTS

1.1	Introduction	2
1.2	Fake news and growing issues	3
1.3	Fake news in journalism and its implications on news values	4
1.4	Journalism and fake news	4
1.5	Use of artificial intelligence and blockchain in checking and mitigating fake news	5
	1.5.1 Artificial intelligence combating fake news	5
	1.5.1.1 Shortcomings of AI	6
	1.5.2 Blockchain combating the fake news	7
	1.5.2.1 Benefits of blockchain-enabled news platforms	8
	1.5.2.2 How does blockchain assist?	9
1.6	Discussions	9
	1.6.1 Deliberating artificial intelligence and fake news	9
	1.6.1.1 Need of the hour	10
	1.6.1.2 AI and syndrome of double-edged sword	12
	1.6.2 Deliberating blockchain and fake news	12
	1.6.2.1 Provenance checking	12
	1.6.2.2 Cutting-edge technology with cautions	14
	1.6.2.3 Solution with using blockchain technology	14
1.7	The way forward	15
References		16

DOI: 10.1201/9781003107767-1

1.1 INTRODUCTION

The traditional definition of news has undergone a metamorphosis; the monopoly of the media organizations as the primary source of news and information has now been replaced by a multidimensional news flow. The news audiences are transforming themselves to digital "prosumers" who not only access news and information online but also share, discuss, and generate their own media content using social networking sites such as blogosphere, YouTube, and Twitter. The online news ecosystem is largely comprised of such user-generated content which is nonmediated, raw, unprocessed, and rich in news values and yet low on credibility and highly susceptible to distortions as it lacks the editorial validation of mainstream journalism. Suffice it to say, editorial validation is essentially related to news values. News values refer to "criteria that influence the selection and presentation of events as published news" (Boyd, 1994). These news values essentially indicate newsworthy (Galtung & Ruge, 1965). These values are not common in nature and differ in diverse cultures. News values of fake news are multidimensional. By definition, generally a fake news report is fulfilling a certain amount of news values such as negativity and conflict (Tsfati et al., 2020). Studies find that even false news reports are going viral and generating good revenues for the media houses (Bakir & McStay, 2018).

Fake news is thriving worldwide especially in India, piggybacking on the social media revolution. The number of social media users has touched a staggering 350 million in the country. The popular messenger app WhatsApp has 400 million active Indian users and has been regarded as the black hole of fake news industry in the country (The Indian Express, 2020). Countermeasures undertaken by the Indian government, such as blocking the access to certain websites and applications aimed at dispelling misinformation on social media platforms, have remained largely incapacitated and met with protests as it contravenes the principles of digital democracy and free speech. Initiatives in India by Alt News, a platform exclusively created to debunk fake news and training sessions organized by Google Lab for Indian journalists to train them in online verification and fact checking, have yielded results in smaller communities (The Economic Times, 2022). However, the wider gamut of social media users remains untouched. Hence, such initiatives need to be replicated on a global scale to yield substantial results. Fake news has made deep inroads into global public communication, in which the countermeasures undertaken by state, media, or academia cannot harness the torrent of disinformation. The role of digital literacy in enhancing citizens' capability to fight against misinformation has become a promising research area in academics and industry worldwide. The traditional media can counter fake news by publishing factual information by debunking the lies and misinformation spread on social media. However, it is seen that media organizations such as television news channels and newspapers harp on such news to create sensational headlines and keep their audiences glued.

1.2 FAKE NEWS AND GROWING ISSUES

Fake news distorts, misleads, and fabricates untruthful information to manipulate the minds of the receiver. It mimics news and is able to influence the public sentiment. It has emerged as a global paradigm among public figures, journalists, and audiences, which has created a sense of distrust and loss of credibility in mainstream media (Lamprou et al., 2021). We live in the posttruth world order where the data are less influential in terms of determining the public opinion in comparison to emotional appeals and beliefs. "Posttruth" and "fake news" are regarded as a cocktail of disinformation and devaluation of facts (Harjuniemi, 2022). Brennen (2017) defined fake news as follows: "Fake news is made-up news, manipulated to look like credible journalistic reports that are designed to deceive us" (p. 180). Disinformation and manipulation of audience's perceptions and opinions have always been parts of our society. During the world wars, radio and newspapers were used to disseminate the state-sponsored propaganda for manipulating public sentiments. However, its impact on media and journalism gradually diminished as media institutions adopted professional and ethical practices such as information verification, evolving sound editorial filtering mechanism, and adhering to the principles of objectivity, fairness, and accuracy in news reporting. However, in the last decade, the proliferation of social media-based, user-generated content has resurfaced the narrative on fake news in the public discourse. The proliferation of digital technology has made it possible for people with vested interests to create and disseminate fake news content, in the form of text, photos, videos, infographics, memes, etc. (McGonagle, 2017). The damaging effect of misinformation and fake news online has become pertinent because of its impact on the socio-political scenario such as political elections and public policy (Abu Arqoub et al., 2022).

Weiss et al. (2020, p. 5) asserted, "While disinformation and propaganda are a willful distortion or misconstruing of fact for the sake of political or physical gain in both times of peace and during warfare, misinformation and rumor are unwitting distortions arising from ignorance and the repeating of erroneous information. This also might fall under the rubric of fake news". Baptista and Gradim (2021) stated that the influx of programmatic web advertising, coupled with ideological motivations, malicious bots, and bad algorithms, constitutes great allies of fake news, promoting the creation of filter bubbles and echo chambers. Facticity and the degree of fake news are the important concepts which explain the fake news (Jahng et al., 2021). Certain aspects of the digital media ecology such as decline of legacy news organizations, the immediacy news cycle, the power and reach of user-generated content, the amplifying effects of the social media, emotional undertone in online content, and the increasing dependency on algorithms by social media and search engines have all contributed to the spread of fake news phenomenon (Schapals & Bruns, 2022).

1.3 FAKE NEWS IN JOURNALISM AND ITS IMPLICATIONS ON NEWS VALUES

Any media outlet or online network that deliberately publishes false information is breaking the rules of good journalism. Furthermore, such devil intentions and the propagation of falsehood through traditional, social, and online media are crimes against humanity that spread chaos, strife, and crises. It flouts the norms of journalistic practice. As information producers and consumers, we are already very familiar with the selection criteria for information and understand why some subjects are attractive and others are not. Furthermore, we can watch how journalists choose their sources and how it influences the public in perceiving the news.

Galtung and Holmboe Ruge (1965) first proposed the idea of news values. Since then, it has undergone multiple revisions in response to the emergence of new journalistic genres and the Internet revolution. However, all the notions of news values hinge on the presumption of accurate information. The fundamental aspect of news is that it bases its message on actual events. Meanwhile, recently, the society has been grappling with the false news.

Fake news is created in a way that makes it appear to be legitimate information. This tendency has detrimental effects outside of the media and communication industries. Its potential effects on education at all levels are even more concerning. Students have long regarded online sources as significant, current, and typically reliable sources of knowledge and data. Distraction from the trustworthiness of news sources undermines the trustworthiness of information sources on the Internet as a whole, which results in fewer reliable network sources for e-learning and education. Although false, erroneous, or distorted information has always existed, it now has immense destructive power because of the Internet. For researchers, media consumers, and educators, understanding how they are created and spread becomes increasingly important.

1.4 JOURNALISM AND FAKE NEWS

Journalism is in crisis; the sea of misinformation is overshadowing it, as the distinction between fake content and factual information is blurred. The immediacy and direct source to audience format of information delivery have disarrayed the traditional role of journalists as gatekeepers (Lamprou et al., 2021). Jahng et al. (2021) studied the US journalists' understanding and perspectives on fake news. The study claims that fake news endorses a particular ideology, which could be manipulating in nature. Fake news is creating the space of existential crisis for journalists and developing a deeper level of distrust among the audiences for the news reports (Richardson, 2017). Needless to say, the traditional role of journalism is to inform, educate, and people. Media has the power in saving the truth from misinformation and facts from fake news.

Currently, journalists rely on a host of digital tools to vet news stories such as reverse image search, verification of the news source and publisher, fact-checking websites, and social media content (Abu Arqoub et al., 2022). The solution to misinformation is good journalism (Richardson, 2017). It is important to train and empower the future journalists who will fight disinformation and uphold the principles of journalism ethics.

The speed and scale at which misinformation multiplies on the WhatsApp platforms make the problem humongous and difficult to curb. A finding reveals that the pace of spreading fake news is faster in Twitter (Vosoughi et al., 2018). Allcott and Gentzkow (2017) have attributed to the cause of making profits and promotion behind faking the news. Journalists have recommended some of the strategies to counter fake news and misinformation such as higher journalistic standards, higher editorial standards, importance to verification, increased transparency in news production, and capacity building of journalists in newer technologies, among others (Schapals & Bruns, 2022). It is pertinent for the journalists to collaborate and engage with audiences to eliminate the suspicion between journalists and audiences (Abu Arqoub et al., 2022). In today's newsrooms, transparency in news production has emerged as a new journalistic norm. However, the scholarly discourse on fake news is western centric.

1.5 USE OF ARTIFICIAL INTELLIGENCE AND BLOCKCHAIN IN CHECKING AND MITIGATING FAKE NEWS

1.5.1 Artificial intelligence combating fake news

Online misinformation is not a new phenomenon. However, it has become more prevalent due to the rapid advancements in ICTs. Fact checking is usually done with manual human interventions. Manual fact checking remains ineffective. Through the automatic detection and elimination of erroneous content, artificial intelligence (AI) offers a potent, scalable, and affordable solution to avoid the skewing of information online, but it also has its own set of restrictions and unexpected consequences. At first appearance, AI seems to offer a neutral defense against misinformation. However, AI systems have their own set of constraints and difficulties, as the next section demonstrates.

Algorithmic Disinformation Detection. AI technologies have been particularly useful in information operations for locating and eliminating questionable, unlawful, and unwanted online content. Bot-spotting and bot-labeling strategies, which use AI, have proven successful in finding and detecting fraudulent bot accounts. Social media companies are assisting the users to determine the credibility of information through bots. Machine-learning algorithms are used by social media outlets to eliminate trolls. The ability to recognize dangerous online conduct is made possible by pattern recognition, which is closely tied to machine learning and AI. AI tools are being used to locate the patterns of false information. Social media networks continue to use the power of algorithms for repetitive tasks.

Fighting the Threat. AI tools can be used to detect and get rid of false information. In fact, over the past few years, AI has successfully been able to discern between human and machine-generated content by recognizing patterns using a variety of algorithms. The ability to classify stances is another feature of some AI-powered analytical tools that can be used to identify whether or not a headline and article body are compatible. By digesting the text and analyzing the writing style, this is accomplished.

Fake news spreads exponentially on social media, which is why Facebook, Google, Twitter, and YouTube have joined the forces to reduce and eradicate it while also promoting official norms on their platforms. Start-ups such as MetaFact have been utilizing AI to track and detect fake news in real time even before COVID-19. The goal of the fact-checking websites is to support the journalists in their efforts to battle fake news but not to replace their labor. By utilizing AI, MetaFact also wants to create a trust layer for the Internet (Sachdev, 2020). The start-up is introducing AI into newsrooms as the first installment of a series to assist journalists in validating news and producing enriched reporting by reducing the cost, time, and effort required to do so with a reduced risk of error. By giving journalists and media organizations direct access to privacy, data interoperability, and cognitive computing expertise, AI tools will support the journalists in their fight against the growing problem of false information.

AI tools can be used to create fake news content easily, and at the same time, they are powerful tools to combat fake news. Deep fakes in particular look enormously realistic and difficult to detect even by the professionals. In the near future, AI-based automated technologies such as algorithms and natural language processing can help users validate the veracity of any information source.

1.5.1.1 Shortcomings of AI

Although AI tools have many advantages, technologies also offer new hazards to democratic political processes and human rights. Scarcity of logical algorithmic applications, invasion of privacy, and changes in contents without the subject's knowledge are some of the issues raised by the expert community. The use of automated tools to identify and combat disinformation has a number of restrictions. The first major flaw in AI's "over inclusiveness" function is the potential overblocking of correct and legal content. Since the technology is constantly evolving, AI tools could be detrimental, which means they sometimes mistakenly identify real information and account as phony. False positives can have a severe effect on the right to free speech and result in the banning of trustworthy and lawful content that is mistakenly classified by machines as misinformation.

The automated systems still have a limited capacity to evaluate the veracity of specific statements. Currently, available AI systems can only recognize straightforward declarative assertions, missing implied claims or claims buried within complicated sentences that are simple for humans to understand. The same holds true for terms that call for certain cultural or environmental information. AI systems are unable to deal with more subtle forms of deception because they have not yet mastered fundamental human notions such as sarcasm and irony. This challenge is made more difficult by linguistic hurdles and national differences in the political and cultural surroundings.

Algorithm bias may result from poor, insufficient, or unrepresentative training data, as well as from the priorities and values of the programmers who create and train the algorithms. AI-based solutions pose crucial considerations regarding who is best suited to decide whether contents are acceptable or unacceptable, legal or unlawful, and desirable or unwanted.

Disruptive technologies are already being used in politics, notably to sway public opinion through the manipulation of information. In particular, four risks stand out: user segmentation and profiling, hyperpersonalized targeting, deep fakes, and people being left out of the loop by AI systems.

As machine-learning technology develops, enemies will be able to recognize people's distinctive traits. A greater problem is presented by the use of AI tools in the production of audio and video material. The so-called "deep fakes", which are incredibly realistic and nearly impossible to tell apart from actual material thanks to digital manipulation, were first employed in the film business.

1.5.2 Blockchain combating the fake news

Blockchain technology is excellent for news verification in a clearly defined, well-organized community with shared values. The use of a suitable consensus mechanism in this community establishes with a very high likelihood for the participants—and for them alone—that the text, approved by a previously designated and trusted body, was not altered by anyone, either intentionally or unintentionally.

Since false news can be used to sway people's opinions for political reasons and to further objectives that are not always in the best interests of society, it has major ramifications for our ideals of democracy, liberty, and society (Allcott & Gentzkow, 2017). When deliberate hoaxes are produced and shared on social media or traditional media, it is called fake news or yellow journalism. Such hoaxes are purposefully constructed to deceive, hurt, and achieve particular political and financial goals. They feature sensational, eye-catching, and false content. The majority of the time, social media users and certain news disseminators report and distribute this type of contents. Blockchain technology is known to revolutionize the information how it is being produced and disseminated (Rijmenam, 2020). Due to the traceability, transparency, and decentralization nature of the blockchain, the issues of disinformation news can be effectively detected and mitigated. The blockchain-enabled platforms can provide online readers with a reliable way of verifying the content and its source.

In the last few years, across the world, a few media and journalism start-ups flourished, which tried to harness the power of blockchain technology and virtual currency to create new business models for journalism. Since the technology of blockchains is based on an accountable and transparent system where the content is unalterable and publishes the original source, this acts as a deterrent to the circulation of fake news.

One such media and journalism start-up is civil, launched in 2017, which envisaged the future sans large media corporations but instead a transparent network of journalists and media consumers investing in cryptocurrencies. The technology that civil utilized was an open-source Ethereum platform based on blockchain. Unfortunately, the media start-up shut down three years later, but it created a new business model, where news consumers supported the journalists and helped create a collaborative platform of transparent and credible journalism. The reputed and independent news agency Associated Press has made its foray in blockchain technologies. It partnered with Chainlink labs in 2021 to make available its trusted economic, sports, and race data on their network. Similarly, it auctioned its first non-fungible token (NFT) artwork on *opensea* an online NFT marketplace and announced its launch in the world of NFT to auction some of the Pulitzer award-winning photographs. Wortheum, considered India's first blockchain-based news and media platform, was launched in 2022. The platform that used a Delegated Proof of Stake (DPoS) protocol aims to monetize media content and empower journalists.

1.5.2.1 Benefits of blockchain-enabled news platforms

News Credibility. The world can determine whether or not the news is phony since the blockchain can bring transparency. The validity of the news will be determined by certain standards such as trust and openness. *News*

Traceability. Blockchain can track the veracity of news going back to its inception, continuing into the future. As a result, the false information can be minimized. *Decentralized Approach.* The issue of fake news can be overcome with a decentralized news platform. Additionally, the lack of centralized data storage guarantees the absence of single arguments of disaster.

1.5.2.2 How does blockchain assist?

Technology features such as distributed consensus, digital signatures, and cryptographic hashing help ensure the permanence and reliability of the original news. The following components make up the media blockchain system in the suggested fix: registration smart contract, identity smart contract update, identity smart contract revoke, and evolvable reputation set.

Blockchain tackles the issue of media outlets changing news or publication dates in the past. This becomes more prominent during the time of election campaigns where the issues of hate speech and libel come to the fore. News sites can improve their transparency with the aid of blockchain platforms, and it will be much simpler and, more importantly, quicker to identify the source of false information. This will not only allow a different end user to confirm the information, but it will also show that each stage's metadata collection was done so. With the technological assistance, the authors can identify people responsible for the development and dissemination before submitting bogus news.

1.6 DISCUSSIONS

1.6.1 Deliberating artificial intelligence and fake news

A socio-technological and multidisciplinary approach is required to combat fake news as solutions depend not only on AI but also on social mechanisms (Shae & Tsai, 2019). In the past few years, blockchain and AI-based applications in the field of media have shown the potential to combat information distortion. AI is a branch of computer science which empowers machines to replicate human capabilities and intelligence. Blockchain is a decentralized technology, based on an encrypted shared database or an immutable ledger, where data are stored securely in blocks and strung together like a chain. It allows information to be recorded and distributed but cannot be altered. As new information or transactions are recorded, they create additional blocks of data without tampering previous records, creating a long history of all transactions that are permanent (Rakheja, 2021). It allows users to access past transaction records and offers a transparent system of sharing and distributing information, without the need for a centralized monitoring and validating authority. Blockchain technology was introduced in 2008, as a public-distributed ledger that powers Bitcoin cryptocurrency. Currently, it has the potential to be a worldwide record keeping system and can be applied across a plethora of domains and sectors (Kaushal, 2022).

1.6.1.1 Need of the hour

The policymakers, communities available on digital social media outlets, fact checkers, and other stakeholders of the society need to work hand in hand to tackle the menace of fake news. There should be a holistic approach to curb the ill effects of false information.

1.6.1.1.1 Correct and downplay false content

The news feed algorithms of social media platforms can be updated to lessen the prominence of false material. Platforms must show effective corrections of content that has been proven inaccurate or misleading in online outlets in addition to reporting and degrading false content. Dissemination of fact-based counter-messages is equally important. Although attribution in online platforms is a challenge, it is crucial to coordinate attribution and response when there is enough evidence to publicly denounce the disinformation perpetrators.

1.6.1.1.2 Encouraging higher accountability and openness

The auditing of AI systems could be used to counteract potential biases in algorithmic decision systems. The data incorporated to develop models must be subjected to further scrutiny thanks to auditing. Ethical design programs are the need of the hour. The algorithmic accountability act is a draught rule that may create the situation of bias and prejudice. The likelihood of biases being introduced into the codes could be reduced by including ethics training. There are growing requests for greater algorithmic transparency in addition to higher accountability. Tech businesses and developers have fiercely opposed such plans, claiming that disclose the source code.

1.6.1.1.3 Deep fakes: Technological countermeasures

Some of the AI experts suggest three technological countermeasures for deep fakes. The first deals with an improved forged material identification utilizing forensic technologies. Tools have been developed for the identification of deep fakes. Microsoft's video authenticator tool helps detect manipulated images and video by generating a confidence score in real time; it analyses the blending boundary of deep fake and subtle greyscale elements that are undetectable to the human eye (Goled, 2020).

1.6.1.1.4 Regulating the content on social media

Policymakers in Europe and America are debating the viability of regulating online material. Current proposals either give governments more control over online content or give platforms more responsibility and liability. The proposed regulations have encountered a variety of difficulties and have been opposed by a number of groups.

The establishment of the roles of various parties associated is a crucial component of the solution. Rebalancing this environment should not entail making online platforms, the jury and judges of what are true. This could result in excessive censorship since platforms might remove legal information out of a lack of prudence and out of concern for the consequences. Governmental regulations can quickly become outdated because technologies frequently advance much more quickly than they do. Growing governmental control over data sometimes prompts worries about laws that can flout civil liberties and provide the government machinery the power to stifle free expression for political reasons.

The conventional regulatory method will not always be effective in a fast-moving world; thus, this needs to be a collective plan among industry, academics, and the government machinery. The multiplicity of Internet businesses necessitates a wide range of suitable regulations and accountability criteria. It would be foolish to advocate for the consistent application of regulations that are one size fits all. Additionally, efforts should be more inclusive.

1.6.1.1.5 Diplomacy and techplomacy

Techplomacy is a term introduced by the Danish government, which refers to technological diplomacy to serve as a bridge between governments and tech companies and fostering trust and cooperation (Norkunas, 2022). By introducing tech delegations or tech ambassadors, nations can foster greater trust among various stakeholders. They can also do this by delegating some of these duties to already existing, pertinent national authorities. *Techplomacy* has the ability to open up new channels for communication and cooperation between the technology industry and governments, taking into account the fact that technology corporations are significant factors affecting global politics (Foremski, 2019). Decision-makers from several nations can utilize this connection to have discussions about things such as election interference, damaging content, disinformation, cybersecurity, and e-evidence for probing the policies.

1.6.1.1.6 Digital and media literacy

Boosting media and digital literacy is a must. Early childhood education should promote digital and media literacy. Children should not just be the focus; electoral officials, senior persons, and marginalized and minority groups should also be considered.

1.6.1.2 AI and syndrome of double-edged sword

The growth of AI tools can prove a double-edged sword for democratic setup. AI tools make human lives better. On the other hand, if rivals use the same technology, they will be able to increase the efficiency and scope of information operations. AI can mobilize digital propaganda which is destructive in nature.

Government policies are frequently displaced by new technologies, which develop much more quickly. Stronger ties, partnerships, and open dialogs between policymakers, engineers, and researchers are required to use appropriate technologies to find solutions to particular problems. Increasing communication among key stakeholders will result in more flexible and realistic policy. There is no one solution to the disinformation problem. In order to combat the upcoming disinformation onslaught, society must be resilient. To promote public awareness and critical media consumption, it is crucial to invest in digital and media literacy. Governments, media outlets, and private entities must collaborate for sustainable solutions for society.

1.6.2 Deliberating blockchain and fake news

Applications of blockchain in the field of media and journalism could help create distributed, transparent networks of reliable media platform (Harrison & Leopold, 2021). It is practically impossible to change information once it has been created using blockchain systems because they employ a decentralized and immutable ledger to record information in a way that is constantly checked and reconfirmed by every party that uses it. Managing the transmission of cryptocurrency such as Bitcoin is one of the most well-known uses of blockchain. However, blockchain has the potential to be a useful tool for tracking not only financial resources but also all types of material. It is becoming possible as blockchain can offer decentralized validation and a transparent chain of custody. Blockchain can be beneficial in detecting digital misinformation.

1.6.2.1 Provenance checking

Tracking and verifying sources and other important information for online media constitute the first method where blockchain may be used to fight misinformation. Publications can utilize blockchain to build a registry of all the photographs they have ever published, allowing anyone to verify metadata such as descriptions, locations, and permissions to be photographed. Varied applications will, of course, have different specifications and forms of pertinent metadata, but generally speaking, blockchain provides a way to confirm the origin of content and any potential manipulations during its digital trip to the final user.

1.6.2.1.1 Maintaining one's online reputation and identity

Traditionally, a piece of content's reputation was mostly derived from its publisher. However, relying solely on institution-based reputation has some serious drawbacks. To make the matters worse, even trustworthy newspapers are increasingly motivated to value interaction over clarity in a digital media environment driven by click-based ad revenue. When readers primarily rely on social media headlines for their news, it can be extremely difficult for them to distinguish between trustworthy news sources and propaganda engines that are motivated by personal interests. Blockchain can be useful in this situation.

Blockchain can also be used to trace the dissemination of content, offering both consumers and publishers more insight into the origins of misinformation and its flow across the online ecosystem. Of course, there are crucial concerns to think about who establishes the standards, who contributes to the ratings, and who handles disagreements with any reputation tracking system. Additionally, in order to comply with national and international regulatory standards, any system created to detect personal data will need to comprise privacy and security best practices. Having said that, since no single, dependable organization is required to make these crucial judgments, the decentralized nature of a blockchain solution can probably assist to allay many of these worries.

1.6.2.1.2 Promoting the use of high-quality content

The fact that content producers and distributors are heavily motivated to get clicks at all costs and that clicks are frequently generated by sensationalized material makes it one of the most difficult parts of spreading accurate information in the contemporary media landscape. Even if ad networks such as Google have pledged to take greater action against false materials, they are still marking their own homework and have no incentive to do so. However, blockchain-based smart contracts provide a way to automate payment for content that has been approved in accordance with predetermined standards of quality.

Of course, the community of stakeholders who establish their standards will always determine how trustworthy these systems are. But if well designed, a blockchain system can cut through the clogged information environment of today and encourage people to exclusively produce and distribute content that complies with community standards. However, it is not a miracle cure.

1.6.2.1.3 More than just technology will be needed to combat disinformation

At the local, state, and central levels, there have already been a number of significant initiatives on the policy front. Blockchain technology has the potential to significantly impact the fight against misinformation, but it is not a panacea. Currently, leaders will be in a good position to create a future that we can all trust if they have the access to the proper combination of education, legislation, and technology.

1.6.2.2 Cutting-edge technology with cautions

One cutting-edge technology, blockchain, has the ability to solve many of the underlying reasons and dangers connected with misinformation and manipulated media as it becomes more and more pervasive online. A blockchain-based system could provide a decentralized, trusted mechanism for confirming the provenance and other significant metadata for online materials. However, it is by no means a panacea. Second, it might make it possible for those who produce and distribute the content to keep their reputations apart from publications and organizations. Finally, it makes it possible to use money as a financial incentive for producing and disseminating material that complies with community-driven criteria for integrity and truth. Blockchain offers a promising starting point to ensure that we can trust the content we see, hear, and watch in an ever-more complicated digital media world. Of course, any technological solution will need to be supplemented by significant policy and education measures.

Deepfakes, incredibly convincing audio, photo, and video content produced by AI, have the potential to cost companies tens of millions of dollars, which is adding gasoline to the fire. And that does not even take into account the less tangible but no less important human effects of technologically enabled deception on society as a whole. The good news is that while technology has exacerbated the issue, it has also created new technologies, namely, blockchain, that may provide a way to address the rising problem of digital disinformation.

1.6.2.3 Solution with using blockchain technology

1.6.2.3.1 Audience

Internet surfers are the modern consumers of mass media, including social media. Initially, users will be those who tend to be early adopters of new technology, but incentives will drive more and more people to the platforms. It is extremely vital to take advantage of tentpole occasions of the year to attract new consumers. Those tentpoles will differ depending on the media organization. An election may be a major event for a news organization; a movie or television premiere may be a tentpole for an entertainment-focused institution.

1.6.2.3.2 Technology

A permissioned blockchain ecosystem with the opportunity to create bridges to open and interoperable blockchains, such as Ethereum, makes up the engage-to-earn paradigm for the media. The project must be able to expand in a safe and controlled environment free from the annoyances of permissionless blockchains, but a path to those permissionless blockchains must also be established for scalability reasons. Incentives will eventually need to stretch beyond the primary ecology. If the tokens can be traded in a permissionless market, their value will increase.

1.6.2.3.3 Identity

It is crucial to present this concept as a fresh and improved method of engaging the audience. It is about being open and reestablishing trust after the fake news years' confidence crisis. Giving users a voice and allowing them to cast votes on organizational choices would help them feel included in the company. Additionally, it is a way to communicate directly with them and restrain the domineering social media companies.

1.7 THE WAY FORWARD

The viral of disinformation of news undermines the credibility of the media and its authority because news is the primary focus of both traditional and online media. As fake news undermines the authority, validity, power, and position of the media, its widespread broadcast challenges the values of the mass communication organs. In addition to self-regulation, which is the greatest professional form of control, governments should enact laws to punish those who spread false information around the world. Humanity suffers a major setback because of disinformation. Fake news also jeopardizes legitimate journalism, professionalism, and journalists' ability to watch over societies and governments on behalf of humanity. In fact, fake news undermines the ability of honest journalism to serve humanity by spreading unchecked misinformation and plunging the globe into an abyss of silence. Fake news not only undermines democracy, but also press freedom, free speech, information democratization, and honest journalism, which might be used to spy on society.

Digital life is enhancing human potential while displacing traditional human tasks. AI algorithms utilized for content generation have produced a highly unsatisfactory situation, where the bogus news spreads like wildfire. In addition, certain media outlets also misrepresent, manipulate, and mislead the audience in order to further their own interests or propaganda. Identifying what is true and what is false is a difficult task, and various fact-checking organizations have attempted to address this issue. However, the problem persists because these fact-checking organizations are run by people or teams who may be biased and require excessive intellectual effort on the part of the individual. Additionally, traditional methods are unable to keep up with the Internet's rapid expansion and the human race's shift to a more digital lifestyle. Many models and frameworks have been offered to deal with fake news identification and its propagation but the platform and model have improved the native models, which employ the machine-learning and blockchain technologies. Everyone is able to post news using this paradigm without intervention from outside sources. This model is scalable in terms of verifying the veracity of the news thanks to the ML techniques used. The suggested model also accepts news files in audio and video formats. This platform is for the people and is user-friendly.

The two disruptive technologies of the Fourth Industrial Revolution (IR4.0) (World Economic Forum, 2016) that have caused significant changes in the market are AI and blockchain. Blockchain technology combined with AI has a lot of promise to develop new business models that are made possible by digitization. Although there is a research on the integration and application of AI and blockchain, our knowledge of the value of this integration for business is yet fragmented.

The high prevalence of fake news is posing very difficult technical, legal, and ethical issues. As a decentralized ledger system, blockchain promises to enable features such as smart contracts, decentralized consensus, and tamper-proof authentication. Blockchain aspires to reconcile emotive interactions with claims of computational truth by acting as a universal governance basis for networked mediation. The measurement and capturing of affect, which inevitably results in an excess that defies interpretation, have been the foundation around which the growth of networks has been based. Blockchain serves as the quintessential example of a techno-democracy fetish because it uses cybernetic self-organizing system principles to undertake political activity in lieu of the subject. It is an affective technology that imitates the painful interaction with the other by acting in our place and absorbing social affect. Precisely, the employment of AI and blockchain technologies in curbing the false news needs to be judicious, keeping the ecology of news media and societal implications in mind.

REFERENCES

Abu Arqoub, O., Abdulateef Elega, A., Efe Özad, B., Dwikat, H., & Adedamola Oloyede, F. (2022). Mapping the scholarship of fake news research: A systematic review. *Journalism Practice, 16*(1), 56–86.

Allcott, H., & Gentzkow, M. (2017). Social media and fake news in the 2016 election. *Journal of Economic Perspectives, 31*(2), 211–36.

Bakir, V., & McStay, A. (2018). Fake news and the economy of emotions: Problems, causes, solutions. *Digital Journalism, 6*(2), 154–175.

Baptista, J. P., & Gradim, A. (2021). "Brave New World" of fake news: How it works. *Javnost-The Public*, 28(4), 426–443.

Boyd, A. (1994). *Broadcast Journalism Techniques of Radio and TV News*. Oxford: Focal Press.

Brennen, B. (2017). Making sense of lies, deceptive propaganda, and fake news. *Journal of Media Ethics*, 32(3), 179–181.

Foremski, T. (2019, February 1). The First Ambassador to Silicon Valley Struggles with 'TechPlomacy,' ZDNet. https://www.zdnet.com/article/danish-ambassador-to-silicon-valley-struggles-with-techplomacy/

Galtung, J., & Ruge, M. H. (1965). The structure of foreign news: The presentation of the Congo, Cuba and Cyprus crises in four Norwegian newspapers. *Journal of Peace Research*, 2(1), 64–90.

Goled, S. (2020). Top AI Based Tools and Techniques for Deepfake Detection. https://analyticsindiamag.com/top-ai-based-tools-techniques-for-deepfake-detection/

Harjuniemi, T. (2022). Post-truth, fake news and the liberal 'regime of truth' – The double movement between Lippmann and Hayek. *European Journal of Communication*, 37(3), 269–283.

Harrison, K., and Leopold, A. (2021). How Blockchain Can Help Combat Disinformation. *Harvard Business Review Online*. https://hbr.org/2021/07/how-blockchain-can-help-combat-disinformation

Jahng, M. R., Eckert, S., & Metzger-Riftkin, J. (2021). Defending the profession: US journalists' role understanding in the era of fake news. *Journalism Practice*, 1–19. DOI: 10.1080/17512786.2021.1919177

Kaushal, T. J. (2022). How Blockchain Will Help India Take a Digital Leap. *Business Today Online*. https://www.businesstoday.in/magazine/30th-anniversary-special/story/how- blockchain-will-help-india-take-a-digital-leap-321692-2022-02-07

Lamprou, E., Antonopoulos, N., Anomeritou, I., & Apostolou, C. (2021). Characteristics of fake news and misinformation in Greece: The rise of new crowdsourcing-based journalistic fact-checking models. *Journalism and Media*, 2(3), 417–439.

McGonagle, T. (2017). "Fake news" false fears or real concerns? *Netherlands Quarterly of Human Rights*, 35(4), 203–209.

Norkunas, Aurelijus (2022, February, 2). What Is Techplomacy—And Is It Actually Needed? *Forbes*. https://www.forbes.com/sites/forbestechcouncil/2022/02/02/what-is-techplomacy---and-is-it-actually-needed/?sh=74f7244e3cdb

Rakheja H. (2021). What Is Blockchain Technology and How Is India Planning to Use It? *Business Standard Online*. https://www.business-standard.com/podcast/technology/what-is- blockchain-technology-and-how-is-india-planning-to-use-it-121110701033_1.html

Richardson, N. (2017). Fake news and journalism education. *Asia Pacific Media Educator*, 27(1), 1–9.

Rijmenam, M. (2020, September 10). How Blockchain Can Prevent the Spread of Fake News. https://www.thedigitalspeaker.com/blockchain-can-prevent-spread-fake-news/

Sachdev, G. (2020, May 20). Artificial Intelligence: A Shield Against 'Fake News'? https://indiaai.gov.in/article/artificial-intelligence-a-shield-against-fake-news

Schapals, A. K., & Bruns, A. (2022). Responding to "fake news": Journalistic perceptions of and reactions to a delegitimising force. *Media and Communication*, 10(3), 5–16.

Shae, Z., & Tsai, J. (2019, July). AI blockchain platform for trusting news. In *2019 IEEE 39th International Conference on Distributed Computing Systems (ICDCS)* (pp. 1610–1619). IEEE.

The Economic Times (2022, May 6). India Has the Most Fact Checkers in the World: Irene Jay Liu, News Lab Lead, APAC at Google. https://economic-times.indiatimes.com/tech/tech-bytes/india-has-the-most-fact-checkers-in-the-world-irene-jay-liu-news-lab-lead-apac-at-google/articleshow/91355596.cms?from=mdr

The Indian Express (2020, March 3). Spot and Stop: 5 Tips to Curb the Menace of Fake News on WhatsApp. https://indianexpress.com/article/technology/social/5-tips-to-spot-and-stop-the-fake-news-on-whatsapp-6296861/

Tsfati, Y., Boomgaarden, H. G., Strömbäck, J., Vliegenthart, R., Damstra, A., & Lindgren, E. (2020). Causes and consequences of mainstream media dissemination of fake news: Literature review and synthesis. *Annals of the International Communication Association*, 44(2), 157–173.

Vosoughi, S., Roy, D., & Aral, S. (2018). The spread of true and false news online. *Science*, 359(6380), 1146–1151.

Weiss, A. P., Alwan, A., Garcia, E. P., & Garcia, J. (2020). Surveying fake news: Assessing university faculty's fragmented definition of fake news and its impact on teaching critical thinking. *International Journal for Educational Integrity*, 16(1), 1–30.

World Economic Forum (2016, January 14). The Fourth Industrial Revolution: What It Means, How to Respond. https://www.weforum.org/agenda/2016/01/the-fourth-industrial- revolution-what-it-means-and-how-to-respond/

Chapter 2

Blockchain technology-based fake news detection

Applications and future research directions

Susheel Yadav
O.P. Jindal Global University

Om Jee Gupta and Sushil Kumar Gupta
Dr. Vishwanath Karad MIT World Peace University

Harish Babu
Indian Institute of Technology (Banaras Hindu University)

CONTENTS

2.1	Introduction	20
2.2	Literature review	21
	2.2.1 Businesses and finance	24
	2.2.2 Supply chain and logistics	25
	2.2.3 Education	25
	2.2.4 Healthcare	25
2.3	Blockchain technology to combat the fake news	26
	2.3.1 By verifying the source of origin of the news	26
	2.3.2 By verifying the content moderation of the news	26
	2.3.3 By tracking the news	26
	2.3.4 By implementing blockchain-based smart contracts for social media users	27
2.4	Challenges in application of blockchain to tackle the fake news	27
	2.4.1 Cost of blockchain implementations	28
	2.4.2 Organisational challenges	29
	2.4.3 Scalability challenges	29
	2.4.4 Regulatory challenges	29
2.5	Conclusions and future research directions	30
References		30

DOI: 10.1201/9781003107767-2

2.1 INTRODUCTION

A false or a misleading information that is reported as news is called fake news. The fake news can be of three major types: partial authentic, deceptive and fabricated (Rubin, 2017). False and misrepresented news reports are nothing new. Since the development of the printing press, it has been a part of media history for a very long time even before the Internet and social media platforms. Internet and social media platforms, however, have offered users the chance to post and share content that spreads swiftly (Chen et al., 2015). The recent, unprecedented spread of online misinformation poses a threat to economy, democracy and society. There are several occasions in the past where fake news or misleading information have impacted the fair elections (Shevtsov et al., 2022; Baptista and Gradim, 2022; Pierri et al., 2020; Bovet and Makse, 2019; Lee, 2019). In various instances during the COVID-19 outbreak, misleading news made it difficult for decision-makers to handle the issue. These instances range from actively promoting the use of hydroxychloroquine to cure the infection, to marketing false remedies such as drinking or gargling heated salt or lemon water and bleach (Chisty et al., 2021; Balakrishnan, 2022; Raza et al., 2022; Shen et al., 2022; Constine, 2020; van Der Linden et al., 2020; Mäkelä, 2021). The risky aspect of fake news is its ability to sway public opinion in one's favour (Rai et al., 2022). Social media platforms have allowed person-to-person communication where one can share the information with the masses (Ahmed and Msughter, 2022; DiMaggio et al., 2001). There is broad agreement among critics that the Internet and social media are the primary factors behind this phenomenon's ubiquity in modern culture. Therefore, Internet and social media are the main enablers of fake news (Alemanno, 2018; De Paor and Heravi, 2020; Bangani, 2021). There are several guidelines, which are issued by the social media platforms, to make their users aware of the fake news. Despite all the efforts by social media companies to increase awareness and teach users how to spot bogus news, many users continue to believe it and share it online.

Fake news has a significant psychological impact on readers, which might lead them to make poor decisions. It may have significant negative financial and health implications. As a result, identifying fake news is extremely important (Shu et al., 2017; Kiahwar and Zafar, 2022). Human judgements are the most popular method of identifying false information; however, they are not always accurate. For a human to correctly identify bogus news, the entire domain must be known (Rubin and Conroy, 2012). In fact, humans are typically ineffective at determining if a piece of news is accurate or not (Giachanou et al., 2022).

Due to these restrictions, a method of automated fake news detection is desperately needed. Knowing who creates fake news and who keeps it going is a significant step towards better understanding the nature of fake news propagating on Internet and social media (Bodaghi and Oliveira, 2022).

Generally, fake news is distributed on social media by the first fake news spreaders, who are not always the fake news' producers. In fact, some social media users will retrieve and share fake news when it is first published by an external source (Bondielli and Marcelloni, 2019). Thus, there are fake news creators and fake news spreaders.

Solutions for preventing the creation and spread of fake news have grown over the past few years as a result of technical development. At the same time, creative approaches of creating and disseminating fake news have also increased. Modern methods based on artificial intelligence (AI), machine learning (ML) and blockchain technologies are being employed as a relatively new research topic for this particular problem as several strategies for countering fake news have been established (Chen et al., 2020).

Blockchain is a recent disruptive technology, which first appeared with reference to Bitcoin (Nakamoto, 2008). Blockchain is a decentralised, immutable database that makes it easier to track digital assets and record transactions in any information network (Narayanan et al., 2016). In essence, blockchain technology (BCT) relies on its own distributed nodes to store, authenticate, deliver and communicate network data (Wei, 2022). Since BCT ensures the accuracy of the data, this particular feature makes it appropriate for use in applications that aim to stop the spread of false information. This chapter focuses on the perspectives of the BCT against the spread of fake news. This study has been explained in the following sections: Section 2.2 presents a detailed literature review regarding blockchain and its applications. Section 2.3 proposes the different aspects of BCT to combat the fake news. In Section 2.4, main challenges in application of blockchain to tackle the fake news are analysed. Finally, Section 2.5 is devoted to the conclusions.

2.2 LITERATURE REVIEW

The literature review was carried out by the authors using the Scopus database. As a huge body of literature on blockchain exists, the researchers used both quantitative and qualitative methods to review the literature for this study. The current study uses bibliometric analysis to determine the volume of the blockchain literature available as part of a quantitative literature review. In fact, bibliometric analysis is a well-established scientific methodology, in which quantitative methods are used to examine bibliometric data, such as publication and citation information (Donthu et al., 2021a; Mukherjee et al., 2021). The approach is also acknowledged as a technique for doing scientific research with applicability in a variety of fields (Donthu et al., 2021b, c; Kumar et al., 2021a, b, c, 2022).

When a simple search using the term "Blockchain" OR "Block-chain" is made in the Scopus database, it resulted in 35,222 documents. When the search results are restricted to articles and book chapters, 13,609

Documents by year

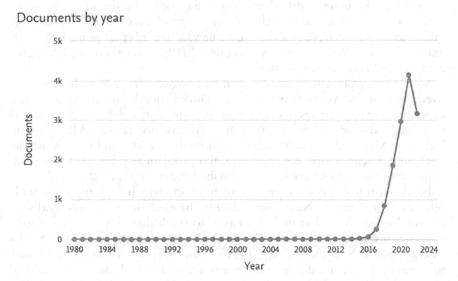

Figure 2.1 Number of documents along with the year of publication.

documents are found. A graph showing the year-wise appearance of these documents is depicted in Figure 2.1. As shown in Figure 2.1, after the year 2016, there is a huge increase in the published documents related to the blockchains. There is a decrease in the documents as the graph was made in the third quarter of 2022. However, there are strong chances that by the time year ends, the trend will continue.

A domain-wise representation of these documents is shown in Figure 2.2, which shows that the blockchain has received the attention from almost all the domains. As this is a technology-related topic, almost half of the documents appeared from the computer science and engineering domain. There is a strong presence in the business and social sciences domains as well. Many of the social issues are being tried to solve through blockchains.

Figure 2.3 represents the top ten countries in terms of origin of publications, China leads in the publications related to the blockchains followed by the United States and India.

A co-occurrence analysis of the author's keywords was carried out to determine the important keywords in the literature. A comma-separated value (.csv) file was retrieved from the Scopus database and used to extract the keywords connected to each article. The co-occurrence network map has been created using the VOSviewer®. A minimum of 50 occurrences were specified as a requirement, and 46 keywords met this standard. These keywords are organised into five clusters as shown in Figure 2.4 and are denoted by various colours. The size of the circle indicates the frequency

Documents by subject area

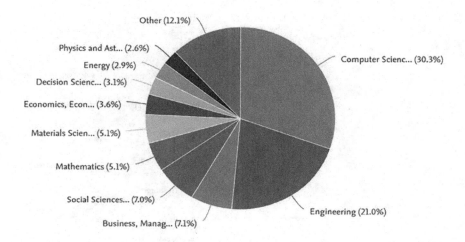

Figure 2.2 Domain-wise representation of the published documents.

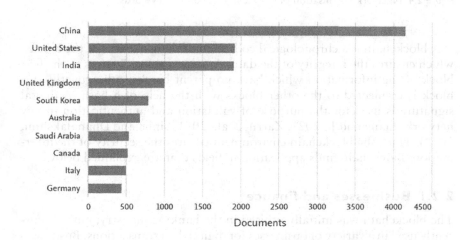

Figure 2.3 Number of documents along with the origin of the documents.

of the keyword occurrence, and the proximity of the circles indicates the co-occurrence of the keywords on this map, which in general displays their co-occurrence (Van Eck and Waltman, 2010, 2014). The readers will find it convenient to search for blockchain-related material using these discovered keywords.

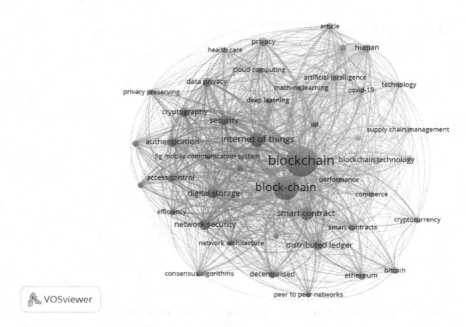

Figure 2.4 Network visualisation of co-occurrence of the keywords.

A blockchain is a chronological collection of the sequences of the blocks, which ensures the integrity of the data. A "genesis block" refers to the first block of the information which have no parent blocks; subsequently, this block is connected to the other blocks with the help of a hash. A digital signature is used for the purpose of validation and authentication in any network (Liang and Ji, 2021; Zarrin et al., 2021; Sinha and Dhanalakshmi, 2022). Thus, the blockchain environment ensures the security of the information. Blockchain finds application in fields that are explained below.

2.2.1 Businesses and finance

The blockchain was initially utilised in the banking industry, but it is currently used in a variety of businesses for digital data transactions. Businesses digitalise their business models to increase their ability to compete in today's dynamic market, with emerging technology, and with shifting consumer demands. Blockchain use in corporate operations has far-reaching effects, such as transaction authentication, disintermediation facilitation, improved efficiency and increased confidence among stakeholders in an organisational ecosystem (Kraemer et al., 2000; Amit and Zott, 2012; Marikyan et al., 2022; Johnson et al., 2008; Morris et al., 2005).

2.2.2 Supply chain and logistics

The blockchain's distributed ledger approach enables diverse supply chain management organisations to participate as nodes to ensure transaction security. The problems with material traceability throughout the process can be successfully resolved by BCT. Blockchain improves supply chain transparency, reducing environmental and social risks and gratifying consumers' growing desire for information access. BCT also has considerable promise for identifying counterfeit goods, streamlining provenance tracing by distributed ledger systems and simplifying paperwork processing for sea freight (De Carvalho et al., 2022; Cole et al., 2019; Saberi et al., 2019; Kersten et al., 2017; Francisco and Swanson, 2018; Abeyratne and Monfared, 2016; McBee and Wilcox, 2020).

2.2.3 Education

The automated management systems of individual higher education institutions or groupings of educational institutions can be upgraded to use blockchain technology. Many institutions, groups and companies are starting their own blockchain investigations to look into the benefits and uses in education. There are some difficulties with record keeping in the traditional educational structure that relies on a centralised system. With the help of blockchain technology, these issues in the education system can be managed in a better way (Liang et al., 2017; Jha and Koul, 2019; Radziwill, 2018; Miah, 2020). Ali et al. (2022) proposed a model based on BCT to make the education sector more efficient.

2.2.4 Healthcare

The BCT uses anonymous transaction recording and validation. This particular feature may be useful in resolving the issue of matching organ donors and receivers using a new cryptographic system that includes carefully managed encryption of private medical data (Canard et al., 2018; Sarier, 2022). Keeping people healthy and ensuring the availability of medical goods are the main objectives of the healthcare supply chain. A supply chain must control the connections between suppliers and customers in order to offer enough customer pleasure at a reasonable price (Xiao et al., 2021; Yaqoob et al., 2019). The supply chain includes all steps of acquiring resources, controlling supplies, and providing goods and services to clients and healthcare workers. Thus, BCT can be handy in managing the healthcare (Bazel et al., 2021; Yaqoob et al., 2019; Xiao et al., 2021).

Besides these applications, blockchain finds extensive use in certification and verifications of information, IoT (Internet of Things), copyrights and royalties.

2.3 BLOCKCHAIN TECHNOLOGY TO COMBAT THE FAKE NEWS

BCT establishes a peer-to-peer secure platform for data storage and exchange while guaranteeing the provenance, authenticity and traceability of data, which make blockchain useful in combating the misinformation (Fraga-Lamas and Fernández-Caramés, 2020). Blockchain has got certain properties which may be very useful for news publishers in combating the misinformation and fake news. A number of different mechanisms are being developed to identify the fake news, as explained below.

2.3.1 By verifying the source of origin of the news

BCT can be used by news publishers to track and validate sources as well as other vital data for online media. By adding ID stamps to published materials, BCT can secure the ownership rights of both authors and publishers. Blockchain can be used by publishers to keep track of all the photographs they've ever released. An effective way to combat fake news is to identify the origin and evolution patterns of fake news. Jang et al. (2018) in their research related to the fake news during the 2016 US presidential election showed that accounts belonging to regular users produced the majority of the fake news-related tweets, although these tweets frequently contained links to shady news websites. Thus, verifying the source news could be the game changer in combating the fake news (Choraś et al., 2021).

2.3.2 By verifying the content moderation of the news

Hisseine et al. (2022) enlisted significant challenges of using social media and the lack of effective method of identifying the moderated content was one of them. Content moderation is not only a problem of the social media platforms itself but when it spreads fake information it becomes a social problem. Hisseine et al. (2022) believe that blockchain can be a solution to identify the content moderation. Since blockchain can trace any changes made to text, image, or video content, giving users of the content the assurance that their content has not been changed (Choraś et al., 2021). Any unauthorised alteration in the information can be detected using the BCT (Srivastava et al., 2021).

2.3.3 By tracking the news

Keeping the record of the news's original source by keeping track of timestamps and the links between various blocks can be helpful in identifying any fake news source. Shang et al. (2018) suggested a process where the relevant content, category and other data are first posted to the blockchain when media outlets write news. The release date, hash and timestamp of the preblock are then recorded as part of the news transmission process so that the chain structure may be created. Third, viewers can identify the source of news by using the blockchain's chain structure and the information that has been saved. Recently, a leading Italian wire service Agenzia Nazionale Stampa Associata (ANSA) has revealed that it would launch a blockchain-based project called "ANSA check" to enable viewers to verify the source of news. It was suggested that by clicking on a tracking label, the technology would enable users to check the veracity of a story.

2.3.4 By implementing blockchain-based smart contracts for social media users

A responsible user of a social media platform can be an asset in combating the fake news or misinformation. By designing and implementing the blockchain-based smart contracts, social media users who are the origin of some information can be held responsible for the information. Social media platforms are used to create and disseminate fake news around the world by their users who contribute stuff to these platforms. However, using blockchain, users must register on the social media platforms with the required information. Smart contract rules will make it easier to grade users based on their information, and if users modify any information on the blockchain network, everyone will be able to see it, making it easier for users to tell whether their content is genuine or edited.

Although detecting fake news may be challenging, the traceability of data, communications architecture and transactions can all be managed with the help of blockchain technology. Blockchain, a relatively new technology, will not necessarily prevent people from uploading fake information, but by making it simpler to track and verify, it could, at the very least, promote a new sense of trust in what they see online.

A summary diagram of blockchain applications in combating the fake news is depicted in Figure 2.5. In the fight against fake news, blockchain's decentralised structure can be quite helpful. Therefore, we should employ BCT to avoid being overwhelmed by lies and untruths.

2.4 CHALLENGES IN APPLICATION OF BLOCKCHAIN TO TACKLE THE FAKE NEWS

The main advantage of BCT is its capacity to operate in a distributed setting with tamper-proof infrastructure. Blockchain is a good tool for battling fake news because of this distinctive trait. The financial industries, including those of real estate, healthcare and law, can all benefit from blockchain

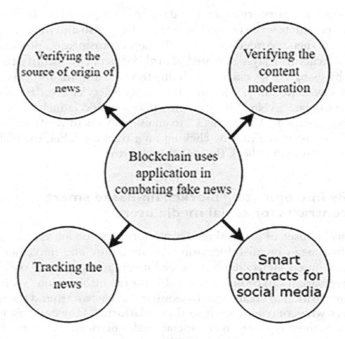

Figure 2.5 Blockchain applications in combating fake news.

technology. However, there will always be a hype phase for new technologies. To overcome every obstacle and use it to drive the modern world, it takes a long time. Even though there are many options, it will still take time to overcome all of the obstacles. The major challenges are discussed below.

2.4.1 Cost of blockchain implementations

BCT is still in its infancy and is not yet fully developed. A reliable blockchain system will require time and effort to develop. The price of hiring a developer to create a blockchain application is just one of the major costs associated with blockchain development. There are also costs associated with the solutions, data migration, onboarding and training. In addition to these expenses, electricity and storage expenses are incurred, depending on the consensus method and other protocols. High electricity prices are associated with blockchain adoption. Proof of work (PoW), one of the consensus methods, uses computational power to confirm the validity of data that are intended to be entered on the blockchain. The price of data storage because of data redundancy is closely tied to this. As blockchain use grows, the system may become slower as a result of the increased data load. Along with cost of the blockchain, another question rises that who shall bear this cost.

2.4.2 Organisational challenges

Blockchains are ecosystems, and in order for them to function properly, it is necessary for widespread adoption throughout an organisation. Not only would an organisation need to implement a blockchain network in order to take advantage of the full capabilities of the blockchain, such as track and trace, but all of its stakeholder organisations would also need to do the same. There are still very few firms who are doing blockchain pilot projects or that have fully deployed the technology. The efficiency and scalability of blockchains will continue to be constrained if they do not first see widespread use. Despite this, there are many reasons to have reason for optimism regarding the increased use of blockchain technology. Organisations are increasingly banding together and forming collaborative blockchain working groups in order to address common pain points and develop solutions that can benefit everyone without disclosing proprietary information. These groups are tasked with developing solutions that can be used by everyone.

2.4.3 Scalability challenges

Implementing BCT presents a number of challenges, one of which is scalability. In practise, blockchains function satisfactorily for a limited number of users. In the past, there have been a few occasions wherein people experienced issues as a result of an increase in the number of users. Certain cryptocurrencies experienced this problem when they had a large number of users on their network; currently, the cryptocurrency developers are struggling to find a solution to the problem. When there are more users on a network, the transitions take longer time to process because of the increased traffic. Because of this, the typical transaction costs are increased, and as a consequence, there are fewer people allowed to utilise the network. It is possible that the entire transaction will take days to be processed. The difficulty in widespread adoption of BCT ultimately results in a decline in the financial potential of the technology. Although some of the blockchain technologies did demonstrate a speedier output to us, these same technologies also showed a slowdown when more people logged into the system.

2.4.4 Regulatory challenges

When deploying BCT in a business, one of the primary challenges that arises is that of regulation. A growing number of businesses are adopting BCT as a method of transaction. However, there are no precise restrictions regarding the regulations themselves. Therefore, when it comes to the blockchain, no one adheres to any particular set of regulations. Now, this is where the problem starts to arise. Despite the fact that blockchain's promise of transparency is one of its advantages, there is still no security. Possibly the only way to get around these obstacles is for governments and other highly regulated industries to come up with blockchain legislation.

2.5 CONCLUSIONS AND FUTURE RESEARCH DIRECTIONS

Using blockchain technology, one can verify the origin, validity and traceability of information, which is helpful in the fight against fake news. This chapter takes a look at some of the characteristics that are now being applied to the fight against false news, as well as those that are being evaluated for potential application in this fight. Even while the BCT has some technological and practical limitations when it comes to combating fake news, the trust mechanisms that it provides can make it more suitable than other technologies for ensuring authenticity and auditing, as well as getting rid of false reality.

Even though blockchain has a tremendous potential to fight fake news, most anti-fake news strategies are still in the conceptualisation stage. It is necessary for news organisations and social media firms to have a comprehensive understanding of how BCT might be effective in the battle against fake news, and there is also a need for widespread acceptance of BCT across organisations. The goal of the research should be to determine whether or not there are successful integration, interoperability and data standards among the different companies. In addition, researchers ought to investigate the practicability of integration strategies for a variety of enterprises located all over the world. Having diverse implementations of blockchain in separate silos creates an existing complexity and interoperability difficulty, which needs to be investigated. It is essential to have a grasp of the legal and regulatory ramifications of blockchain interoperability, particularly in light of the fact that concerns around security and privacy are relevant issues.

Researchers are beginning to become aware of the technical restrictions that are associated with the storing of data on the blockchain, and researchers are also beginning to investigate potential alternatives.

The most crucial step is to educate the general public about the benefits that may be gained by using blockchain technology. The negative opinion that the general public has of blockchain applications, such as cryptocurrencies, is one factor that contributes to user resistance which needs to be clarified.

REFERENCES

Abeyratne, S. A., & Monfared, R. P. (2016). Blockchain ready manufacturing supply chain using distributed ledger. *International Journal of Research in Engineering and Technology*, 5(9), 1–10.

Ahmed, M. O., & Msughter, A. E. (2022). Assessment of the spread of fake news of Covid-19 amongst social media users in Kano State, Nigeria. Computers in Human Behavior Reports, 6, 100189.

Alemanno, A. (2018). How to counter fake news? A taxonomy of anti-fake news approaches. *European Journal of Risk Regulation*, 9(1), 1–5.

Ali, S. I. M., Farouk, H., & Sharaf, H. (2022). A blockchain-based models for student information systems. *Egyptian Informatics Journal*, 23(2), 187–196.

Amit, R., & Zott, C. (2012). Creating value through business model innovation. *MIT Slogan Management Review*, 53, 41–49.

Balakrishnan, V. (2022). COVID-19 and fake news dissemination among Malaysians–Motives and its sociodemographic correlates. *International Journal of Disaster Risk Reduction*, 73, 102900.

Bangani, S. (2021). The fake news wave: Academic libraries' battle against misinformation during COVID-19. *The Journal of Academic Librarianship*, 47(5), 102390.

Baptista, J. P., & Gradim, A. (2022). Online disinformation on Facebook: The spread of fake news during the Portuguese 2019 election. *Journal of Contemporary European Studies*, 30(2), 297–312.

Bazel, M. A., Mohammed, F., & Ahmed, M. (2021, August). Blockchain technology in healthcare big data management: Benefits, applications and challenges. In *2021 1st International Conference on Emerging Smart Technologies and Applications (eSmarTA)* (pp. 1–8). IEEE.

Bodaghi, A., & Oliveira, J. (2022). The theater of fake news spreading, who plays which role? A study on real graphs of spreading on Twitter. *Expert Systems with Applications*, 189, 116110.

Bondielli, A., & Marcelloni, F. (2019). A survey on fake news and rumour detection techniques. *Information Sciences*, 497, 38–55.

Bovet, A., & Makse, H. A. (2019). Influence of fake news in Twitter during the 2016 US presidential election. *Nature Communications*, 10(1), 1–14.

Canard, S., Pointcheval, D., Santos, Q., & Traoré, J. (2018, July). Privacy-preserving plaintext-equality of low-entropy inputs. In *International Conference on Applied Cryptography and Network Security* (pp. 262–279). Springer, Cham.

Chen, Q., Srivastava, G., Parizi, R. M., Aloqaily, M., & Al Ridhawi, I. (2020). An incentive-aware blockchain-based solution for internet of fake media things. *Information Processing & Management*, 57(6), 102370.

Chen, X., Sin, S. C. J., Theng, Y. L., & Lee, C. S. (2015). Why students share misinformation on social media: Motivation, gender, and study-level differences. *The Journal of Academic Librarianship*, 41(5), 583–592.

Chisty, M. A., Islam, M. A., Munia, A. T., Rahman, M. M., Rahman, N. N., & Mohima, M. (2021). Risk perception and information-seeking behavior during emergency: An exploratory study on COVID-19 pandemic in Bangladesh. *International Journal of Disaster Risk Reduction*, 65, 102580.

Choraś, M., Demestichas, K., Giełczyk, A., Herrero, Á., Ksieniewicz, P., Remoundou, K., … & Woźniak, M. (2021). Advanced Machine Learning techniques for fake news (online disinformation) detection: A systematic mapping study. *Applied Soft Computing*, 101, 107050.

Cole, R., Stevenson, M., & Aitken, J. (2019). Blockchain technology: Implications for operations and supply chain management. Supply Chain Management, 24(4), 469–483.

Constine, J. (2020). Facebook Deletes Brazil President's Coronavirus Misinfo Post. Tech Crunch.

De Carvalho, P. R., Naoum-Sawaya, J., & Elhedhli, S. (2022). Blockchain-enabled supply chains: An application in fresh-cut flowers. *Applied Mathematical Modelling*, 110, 841–858.

De Paor, S., & Heravi, B. (2020). Information literacy and fake news: How the field of librarianship can help combat the epidemic of fake news. *The Journal of Academic Librarianship*, 46(5), 102218.

DiMaggio, P., Hargittai, E., Neuman, W. R., & Robinson, J. P. (2001). Social implications of the Internet. *Annual Review of Sociology*, 27, 307–336.

Donthu, N., Kumar, S., Mukherjee, D., Pandey, N., & Lim, W. M. (2021a). How to conduct bibliometric analysis: An overview and guidelines. *Journal of Business Research*, 133, 285–296.

Donthu, N., Kumar, S., Pandey, N., Pandey, N., & Mishra, A. (2021b). Mapping the electronic word-of-mouth (eWOM) research: A systematic review and bibliometric analysis. *Journal of Business Research*, 135, 758–773.

Donthu, N., Kumar, S., Pattnaik, D., & Lim, W. M. (2021c). A bibliometric retrospection of marketing from the lens of psychology: Insights from psychology & marketing. *Psychology & Marketing*, 38(5), 834–865.

Fraga-Lamas, P., & Fernández-Caramés, T. M. (2020). Fake news, disinformation, and deepfakes: Leveraging distributed ledger technologies and blockchain to combat digital deception and counterfeit reality. *IT Professional*, 22(2), 53–59.

Francisco, K., & Swanson, D. (2018). The supply chain has no clothes: Technology adoption of blockchain for supply chain transparency. *Logistics*, 2(1), 2.

Giachanou, A., Ghanem, B., Ríssola, E. A., Rosso, P., Crestani, F., & Oberski, D. (2022). The impact of psycholinguistic patterns in discriminating between fake news spreaders and fact checkers. *Data & Knowledge Engineering*, 138, 101960.

Hisseine, M. A., Chen, D., & Yang, X. (2022). The application of blockchain in social media: A systematic literature review. *Applied Sciences*, 12(13), 6567.

Jang, S. M., Geng, T., Li, J. Y. Q., Xia, R., Huang, C. T., Kim, H., & Tang, J. (2018). A computational approach for examining the roots and spreading patterns of fake news: Evolution tree analysis. *Computers in Human Behavior*, 84, 103–113.

Jha, S., & Koul, S. (2019, January). Application of block chain technology in higher education. In 16th AIMS Int'l Conference on Management (AIMS–16).

Johnson, M. W., Christensen, C. M., & Kagermann, H. (2008). Reinventing your business model. *Harvard Business Review*, 86(12), 57–68.

Kersten, W., Blecker, T., & Ringle, C. M. (2017). *Digitalization in supply chain management and logistics: Smart and digital solutions for an industry 4.0 environment*. Berlin: epubli GmbH.

Kiahwar, A., & Zafar, A. (2022). Fake News Detection on Pakistani news using machine learning and deep learning. Available at SSRN 4090739.

Kraemer, K. L., Dedrick, J., & Yamashiro, S. (2000). Refining and extending the business model with information technology: Dell Computer Corporation. *The Information Society*, 16(1), 5–21.

Kumar, S., Lim, W. M., Pandey, N., & Westland, J. C. (2021a). 20 years of electronic commerce research. *Electronic Commerce Research*, 21(1), 1–40.

Kumar, S., Lim, W. M., Sivarajah, U., & Kaur, J. (2022). Artificial intelligence and blockchain integration in business: Trends from a bibliometric-content analysis. *Information Systems Frontiers*, 1–26. https://doi.org/10.1007/s10796-022-10279-0

Kumar, S., Pandey, N., Lim, W. M., Chatterjee, A. N., & Pandey, N. (2021b). What do we know about transfer pricing? Insights from bibliometric analysis. *Journal of Business Research*, 134, 275–287.

Kumar, S., Sureka, R., Lim, W. M., Kumar Mangla, S., & Goyal, N. (2021c). What do we know about business strategy and environmental research? Insights from Business Strategy and the Environment. *Business Strategy and the Environment.* https://doi.org/10.1002/bse.2813

Lee, T. (2019). The global rise of "fake news" and the threat to democratic elections in the USA. *Public Administration and Policy*, 22(1), 15–24.

Liang, W., & Ji, N. (2021). Privacy challenges of IoT-based blockchain: A systematic review. *Cluster Computing*, 25, 1–19.

Liang, X., Shetty, S., Tosh, D., Kamhoua, C., Kwiat, K., & Njilla, L. (2017, May). Provchain: A Blockchain-based data provenance architecture in cloud environment with enhanced privacy and availability. In *2017 17th IEEE/ACM International Symposium on Cluster, Cloud and Grid Computing (CCGRID)* (pp. 468–477). IEEE.

Mäkelä, T. (2021). Response strategies of platform companies during COVID-19 crisis: A case study of Facebook and Google. Master's program Industrial Engineering and Management, Helsinki.

Marikyan, D., Papagiannidis, S., Rana, O. F., & Ranjan, R. (2022). Blockchain: A business model innovation analysis. *Digital Business*, 2(2), 100033.

McBee, M. P., & Wilcox, C. (2020). Blockchain technology: Principles and applications in medical imaging. *Journal of Digital Imaging*, 33(3), 726–734.

Miah, M. (2020). Blockchain technology in peer-to-peer elearning: Opportunities and challenges. In *Proceedings of the EDSIG Conference ISSN* (Vol. 2473, p. 4901).

Morris, M., Schindehutte, M., & Allen, J. (2005). The entrepreneur's business model: Toward a unified perspective. *Journal of Business Research*, 58(6), 726–735.

Mukherjee, D., Kumar, S., Donthu, N., & Pandey, N. (2021). Research published in management international review from 2006 to 2020: A bibliometric analysis and future directions. *Management International Review*, 61(5), 599–642.

Nakamoto, S. (2008). A peer-to-peer electronic cash system. Bitcoin. https://bitcoin. org/bitcoin.pdf, 4, 2.

Narayanan, A., Bonneau, J., Felten, E., Miller, A., & Goldfeder, S. (2016). *Bitcoin and Cryptocurrency Technologies: A Comprehensive Introduction.* Princeton, NJ: Princeton University Press.

Pierri, F., Artoni, A., & Ceri, S. (2020). Investigating Italian disinformation spreading on Twitter in the context of 2019 European elections. *PloS One*, 15(1), e0227821.

Radziwill, N. (2018). Blockchain revolution: How the technology behind Bitcoin is changing money, business, and the world. *The Quality Management Journal*, 25(1), 64–65.

Rai, N., Kumar, D., Kaushik, N., Raj, C., & Ali, A. (2022). Fake News Classification using transformer based enhanced LSTM and BERT. *International Journal of Cognitive Computing in Engineering*, 3, 98–105.

Raza, M. A., Nor, F. M., & Mehmood, R. (2022). Reading habits of medical practitioners: Young doctors in Pakistan, a case study. *Journal of Taibah University Medical Sciences*, 17, 844–852.

Rubin, V. L. (2017). Deception detection and rumor debunking for social media. In *The SAGE Handbook of Social Media Research Methods* (p. 342). London: SAGE.

Rubin, V. L., & Conroy, N. (2012). Discerning truth from deception: Human judgments and automation efforts. *First Monday*, 17(5).

Saberi, S., Kouhizadeh, M., Sarkis, J., & Shen, L. (2019). Blockchain technology and its relationships to sustainable supply chain management. *International Journal of Production Research*, 57(7), 2117–2135.

Sarier, N. D. (2022). Privacy preserving biometric authentication on the blockchain for smart healthcare. *Pervasive and Mobile Computing*, 101683. https://doi.org/10.1016/j.pmcj.2022.101683

Shang, W., Liu, M., Lin, W., & Jia, M. (2018, June). Tracing the Source of News Based on Blockchain. In *2018 IEEE/ACIS 17th International Conference on Computer and Information Science (ICIS)* (pp. 377–381). IEEE.

Shen, Z., Zhong, Z., Xie, J., Zhang, Q., & Li, S. (2022). The effects of information-seeking behaviors on risk perception during the COVID-19 pandemic: A cross-sectional correlational survey. *Psychology Research and Behavior Management*, 15, 1707.

Shevtsov, A., Tzagkarakis, C., Antonakaki, D., & Ioannidis, S. (2022, May). Identification of Twitter Bots Based on an Explainable Machine Learning Framework: The US 2020 Elections Case Study. In *Proceedings of the International AAAI Conference on Web and Social Media* (Vol. 16, pp. 956–967).

Shu, K., Sliva, A., Wang, S., Tang, J., & Liu, H. (2017). Fake news detection on social media: A data mining perspective. *ACM SIGKDD Explorations Newsletter*, 19(1), 22–36.

Sinha, B. B., & Dhanalakshmi, R. (2022). Recent advancements and challenges of Internet of Things in smart agriculture: A survey. *Future Generation Computer Systems*, 126, 169–184.

Srivastava, S., Kumar, A., Jha, S. K., Dixit, P., & Prakash, S. (2021). Event-driven data alteration detection using block-chain. *Security and Privacy*, 4(2), e146.

van Der Linden, S., Roozenbeek, J., & Compton, J. (2020). Inoculating against fake news about COVID-19. *Frontiers in psychology*, 11, 566790.

Van Eck, N. J., & Waltman, L. (2010). Software survey: VOSviewer, a computer program for bibliometric mapping. *Scientometrics*, 84, 523–538.

Van Eck, N. J., & Waltman, L. (2014). Visualizing bibliometric networks. In *Measuring Scholarly Impact: Methods and Practice* (pp. 285–320). Springer.

Wei, D. (2022). Gemiverse: The blockchain-based professional certification and tourism platform with its own ecosystem in the metaverse. *International Journal of Geoheritage and Parks*, 10(2), 322–336.

Xiao, Y., Xu, B., Jiang, W., & Wu, Y. (2021). The HealthChain blockchain for electronic health records: Development study. *Journal of Medical Internet Research*, 23(1), e13556.

Yaqoob, S., Khan, M. M., Talib, R., Butt, A. D., Saleem, S., Arif, F., & Nadeem, A. (2019). Use of blockchain in healthcare: A systematic literature review. *International Journal of Advanced Computer Science and Applications*, 10(5).

Zarrin, J., Wen Phang, H., Babu Saheer, L., & Zarrin, B. (2021). Blockchain for decentralization of internet: Prospects, trends, and challenges. *Cluster Computing*, 24(4), 2841–2866.

Chapter 3

Deep learning-based intelligent systems for audio abuse prediction

A survey

Kaustubh V. Sakhare
Lear Corporation

Radhika V. Kulkarni
Pune Institute of Computer Technology

CONTENTS

3.1 Introduction   35
3.2 Related work   38
3.3 Research methodology   42
3.4 Conclusion   43
References   44

3.1 INTRODUCTION

People must articulate themselves by utilizing the proper forms of communication in the pursuit of sustainable society, and thus, healthy communication is essential for establishing connections between individuals (Genç, 2017). Nowadays, one of the most well-known ways to express one's opinions is through social media platforms. These discussion forums enable the comparison of various viewpoints and the exchange of facts and opinions on any subject. In any episode, it may be challenging to maintain fairness and an acceptable standard of conduct on these forums these days. On these platforms, a number of poisonous, hostile, and abusive communication styles have been accepted, adversely affecting a person's psychological and mental health. This can occasionally have detrimental, long-lasting effects on the individual. Such situations can harm anyone, prohibit them from expressing their feelings, completely alienate them, and cause them to stop asking for and accepting aid from others. Increased use of vulgar language, cyber bullying, racial slurs, and other repressive behaviors are typical examples that demand our attention for effective communication.

Figure 3.1 depicts the statistics of cyber bullying among children on different digital platforms, as recently reported by McAfee (*Cyberbullying*

DOI: 10.1201/9781003107767-3

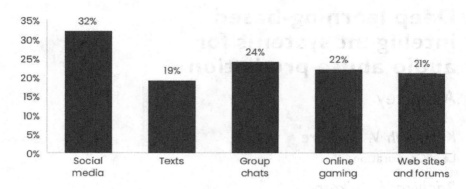

Figure 3.1 Cyberbullying among children on different digital platforms (*Cyberbullying in Plain Sight – A McAfee Connected Family Report*, 2022).

Figure 3.2 Nation-wise statistics of racist cyberbullying (*Cyberbullying in Plain Sight – A McAfee Connected Family Report*, 2022).

in Plain Sight – A McAfee Connected Family Report, 2022). This report states that the racist cyberbullying, reaching 34% in the United States and 42% in India, posed this threat most visibly in these two countries. It is shown in Figure 3.2. As per the report by the Pew Research Center in the United States (*The State of Online Harassment*, n.d.), which is referenced in Figure 3.3, more than 60% of Americans have experienced online harassment and abuse on social media. Despite the fact that different people are attacked online for a variety of reasons or features, it has been discovered that, on the whole, women are more emotionally or mentally affected by online hate speech or abuse than men. Women have stated that episodes of online abuse are particularly upsetting for them, according to a poll by the Pew Research Center, as shown in Figure 3.4.

Abuse is now universally acknowledged as posing a serious threat to society. With the contents reaching a large audience quickly in the current internet age, the problem of abuse becomes even more significant (Ashraf, 2020). Currently, there is nasty content everywhere, including in audio chat rooms and social networking forums. Such material leads to cyber bullying,

Adults under 30 are more likely than any other age group to report experiencing any form of harassment online

% of U.S. adults who say they have personally experienced the following behaviors online

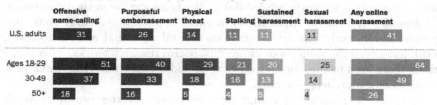

Note: Those who did not give an answer are not shown.
Source: Survey of U.S. adults conducted Sept. 8-13, 2020.
"The State of Online Harassment."

PEW RESEARCH CENTER

Figure 3.3 Online hate survey conducted in 2020 for adults in the United States (*The State of Online Harassment*, n.d.).

Women targeted in online harassment are more than twice as likely as men to say most recent incident was very or extremely upsetting

Among the 41% of U.S. adults who have personally experienced online harassment, % who say their most recent experience was ___ upsetting

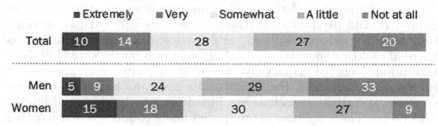

Note: Those who did not give an answer are not shown.
Source: Survey of U.S. adults conducted Sept. 8-13, 2020.
"The State of Online Harassment"

PEW RESEARCH CENTER

Figure 3.4 Mental health of women's statistics (*The State of Online Harassment*, n.d.).

which in turn produces disgusting behavior, misrepresentation, and even murder. Because of the widespread usage of digital/social media applications, identifying hate/abusive media online has received a lot of attention (MacAvaney et al., 2019).

Deep learning frameworks are already being targeted to control abusive and nasty image and text content to a considerable extent. The development of a detection technique that could control and identify such offensive audio remarks is urgently needed due to the fast increase in the penetration of digital/social media applications in audio applications. Aural abuse has gotten significantly less attention than textual or visual abuse; however, both have been the subjects of numerous, useful research works. This chapter is motivated to present an overview of audio abuse detecting intelligent systems based on deep learning.

Section 3.2 presents a comprehensive survey of the prevalent work done in the audio abuse detection. Section 3.3 comprehends the standard research methodology for deep learning-based intelligent system for audio abuse detection. Section 3.4 concludes the article and points toward the future research paradigm.

3.2 RELATED WORK

According to reports, as internet usage has expanded, cyber bullying, cyber hatred, and other cybercrimes have been on the rise. The issue of online abuse has become more widespread than it was in the previous decade, according to numerous data records, and it is expected to get worse as more people become aware of it. These online abuse posts or tweets may contain any combination of text, voice, video, or even pictures. Online abuse has caused many people to experience mental, emotional, and psychological issues. Sometimes it has triggered riots, argumentative debates, killings, or even suicides. Consequently, it is essential to create some strategies that could prevent the spread of these harmful messages or articles. To prevent these posts from appearing in our social media feeds, the social media company has been adopting a variety of strategies, such as machine learning algorithms or human moderators. There are now many studies being conducted that have led to results in terms of locating and minimizing the harmful textual or visual contents that are prevalent on social media platforms. It is achievable using a variety of deep learning techniques. Lack of true data, which is commonly caused by information being artificially created to feed the model, is the main barrier to doing such research inquiries. To prohibit such bad contents from spreading, organizations such as Meta and Twitter are actively working to identify it on their network. As we have seen, though, bias and a host of other factors can affect whether hate speech gets removed.

The majority of recent research is focused on finding abusive/hate speech in textual data in both monolingual and multilingual situations (Aluru et al., 2020; Ayo et al., 2020; Bosco et al., 2018; Davidson et al., 2017;

Holkar et al., 2020; Lynn et al., 2019; MacAvaney et al., 2019; Mathew et al., 2020; Mollas et al., 2022; Orts, 2019; Ousidhoum et al., 2019; Roy et al., 2020; Safaya et al., 2020). The addition of multimedia datasets has sped the identification of abusive content on images and videos (Alcântara et al., 2020; Ashraf et al., 2022; Gangwar et al., 2017; Hossain Junaid et al., 2021; Kiela et al., 2020; Kumar et al., 2021). Although the detection of abusive content in text, image, and video formats is addressed by many researchers, the audio modality has received less attention due to the following major challenges:

- Scarcity of benchmark datasets for experimentation.
- Audio preprocessing.
- Audio quality and differences in tone, dialect, style, and surroundings.
- Need of highly accurate automatic speech recognition/audio-to-text system.
- Only keyword spotting approach to detect abusive words is less effective as contextual knowledge is equally important.
- Template matching is challenging because of neologism, irregularity, and multilingualism.

The deep learning approach has been employed by the research community for dealing with the crucial task of abusive content identification in audio data. It implements the convolutional neural network (CNN), recurrent neural network (RNN) with gated recurrent units (GRUs), and long short-term memory (LSTM) for developing the intelligent systems for recognizing audio abuse. Transfer learning (Pan & Yang, 2010) is a popular approach for hate speech detection (Ali et al., 2022; Bigoulaeva et al., 2021; Lu et al., 2020; Mozafari et al., 2019; Touahri & Mazroui, 2022) as it employs a pretrained model to solve the problems of same type, thus resulting in higher performance while cutting down on training time. Also, it does not need the extensive usage of data. Hence, to predict abusive content in audios, transfer learning is preferred by many researchers (Rahut et al., 2020; Rana & Jha, 2022; Sharon et al., 2022). Audio abuse analysis needs consideration of underlying emotions and textual semantics in abusive audio. It thus demands multimodal learning strategy that makes use of three crucial aspects of the information included in the audios: (1) auditory content, (2) the emotions that are conveyed in them, and (3) the waveform's textual semantics. The work based on multimodal learning employs end-to-end modalities for different languages, extracts the characteristics for each modality using modality-specific models, and then combines the modalities to see significant gains (Rana & Jha, 2022; Sharon et al., 2022; Sutejo & Lestari, 2019). Table 3.1 lists the different research studies carried out by the researcher related to abuse and online hate analysis in audios.

Table 3.1 Online abuse and hate analysis related work

Sr. No.	Reference	Dataset	Purpose	Methodology
1	Ablaza et al., (2014)	Thirty speakers are randomly selected giving recordings of sentences may or may not be having disrespectful words	Identifying irrelevant words treating 10 in number at time and suppressing them	Multilayer perceptron (MLP) classifier with hidden Markov model (HMM) decoder
2	Sutejo and Lestari (2019)	Indonesian language text and audio data collected from social media	Hate speech detection in Indonesian language text and audio	Textual model using LSTM, acoustic model using openSMILE toolkit, multimodal model
3	Rahut et al. (2020)	Bengali speech recorded with 960 Bengali individuals	Abusive and nonabusive speech classification is done using transfer learning	Transfer learning for feature extraction and classifiers such as linear support vector, multilayer perceptron, and multinomial naïve Bayes
4	Holkar et al. (2020)	Kaggle dataset: lethal comment. The classification is as follows: severe toxic, obscene, threat, identity-hate, toxic, insult classes	Identification of abusive or lethal comments	FastText, Word2Vec, CNN
5	Wu and Bhandary (2020)	Videos	Hate speech detection in videos	Audio extraction from videos, speech-to-text conversion, and classifiers like random forest

(Continued)

Table 3.1 (Continued) Online abuse and hate analysis related work

Sr. No.	Reference	Dataset	Purpose	Methodology
6	Yousefi and Emmanouilidou (2021)	(1) Short audios collected from online multiplayer gaming platforms (2) IEMOCAP (Busso et al., 2008)	Toxic language classification based on the complete acoustical context of the utterance	Self-attentive convolutional neural networks (CNNs)
7	Boishakhi et al. (2021)	Dataset collected from web series with hate speech and dialogs	Hate speech detection in video	Machine learning and natural language processing
8	Gupta et al. (2022)	ShareChat's audio chatroom dataset is used, which is recorded in multiple Indian languages	Abuse chat detection from the audio dataset	VGG (Hershey et al., 2017), Wav2Vec2 (Baevski et al., 2020), recurrent neural network (RNN) with gated recurrent units (GRU) and long short-term memory (LSTM)
9	Sharon et al. (2022)	ShareChat's audio chatroom dataset is used, which is recorded in multiple Indian languages	Multiple modalities are considered such as audio, emotion, and text as an extension of the work by same research group	Wav2Vec2 (Baevski et al. 2020), Emotion encoder using the librosa library (McFee et al. 2015), text encoder using Sentence-BERT (Reimers & Gurevych, 2019), Classification using (1) ADIMA (Gupta et al., 2022) and (2) stack classifier
10	Rana and Jha (2022)	(1) Hate Speech Detection Video Dataset (HSDVD), (2) IEMOCAP, and (3) Twitter	Hate speech detection using semantic and emotion features	Multimodal deep learning using semantic and emotion features: (1) semantic learning using BERT (Reimers & Gurevych, 2019) and ALBERT (Wiedemann et al. 2020) and (2) emotion prediction using multitask learning (MTL) model

3.3 RESEARCH METHODOLOGY

Figure 3.5 depicts the standard research methodology for deep learning-based intelligent system to classify the audio chats and get the desired classification results based on abusive and nonabusive contents. The segregation of audio from a multimodal social media post requires careful effort, as separating only the words is not enough to establish the semantic relationship between them. This semantic understanding is crucial for inferring whether the content is vulnerable and classifying it as abusive or nonabusive.

The growing interest in audio abuse detection has led to the creation of a plethora of datasets from sources such as ShareChat and Twitter. Twitter dataset is one of the popular selections by the researchers as this microblogging platform is closest to the target multimedia domain consisting of video/audio blogs. Similarly, ShareChat is one of the most popular social media platforms supporting more than 10 regional languages in India. The ShareChat application team developed the dataset, which is openly accessible for upcoming academic studies. The collection includes Bengali, Bhojpuri, Gujarati, Haryanvi, Hindi, Kannada, Malayalam, Odia, Punjabi, and Tamil language audio samples taken from the application's public chat rooms and is very diversified in nature.

All the datasets were subjected to the same preprocessing step as stereo audio to mono audio conversion, mono audio to spectrogram converter, and feature extraction using deep learning algorithms. Audio signal processing being one of the demanding domains for spectral representation, it presents the waveforms using the graphical representation of sound plotted as time versus amplitude. Once the spectral representation is achieved, Mel-frequency cepstral coefficients (MFCCs) (Ganchev et al., 2005) give the change in the spectral representation of the audio signals. Multiple

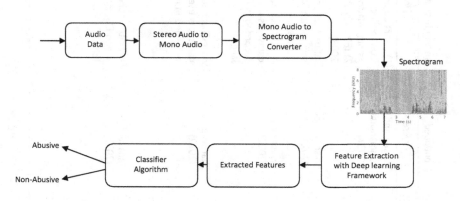

Figure 3.5 Standard research methodology.

characteristics are initially collected from the dataset and supplied into the base model pertaining to process the audio signals. The MFCC features depict the geometry of the vocal tract as well as the distinctive sound units known as phonemes. The high-level steps in MFCC algorithm involve (1) transforming the audio dataset's analog signal into a digital signal, (2) pre-emphasis, (3) windowing, (4) discrete Fourier transform, (5) Mel spectrum, and (6) discrete cosine transformation.

For performing feature extraction from spectrograms, various transfer-learning modules can be tried out. One of the renowned pretrained neural network models is VGG16 (Hershey et al., 2017). The popular VGG16 transfer-learning models are devised on open-source image datasets. This benchmark of the deep learning pretrained models can be used to replace the conventional models based on the audio feature extraction and machine learning classifiers for audio abuse detection. Multimodal deep learning models would prove inclusive to classify abusive content in audio using spectral features, forming a semantic relation in the overall context of the conversation, and representing those in the deep neural-based feature planes. Various performance measures such as accuracy, precision, recall, sensitivity, specificity, F1 score, and area under curve (AUC) are used to evaluate the deep learning-based prediction model.

3.4 CONCLUSION

Social media use is increasing everyday, making miracles in the social life of an individual and value addition in academic, cultural, and many more aspects. It is only natural that a sizeable section of the public makes frequent use of these social media platforms. There is still a lot of work to be done, despite the social media platforms' diligent efforts to filter their postings and feeds to foster favorable user experiences. Nevertheless, some selected work is seen in audio abuse detection, majority of the previous research are carried out using conventional audio feature extraction and machine learning-based classifier design. The current era of the farthest deep learning-based framework simplifies the task of abuse detection in audio. Vulnerability in the audio/speech is comparatively fiddly to analyze as not only the word but also the semantic analysis needs to be performed after the use of those words in the conversation. The prevalent work and survey restrict the scope of the research toward identification of such abusive keywords. Indeed, this article foresees the necessity to establish the relationship between different words and generate the most appropriate and nearing meaning out of the whole conversation. Compared to the earlier shallow approaches of abusive word identification, the consideration of audio quality and differences in tone, dialect, style, and surroundings necessitates the spectral representation of audio. This intrinsic attribute when conglomerated with the multimodalities leads to deeper feature representations. Each dataset has its advantages, but at the same time, it suffers from unintended biases. This complexity houses the multiple combinations of datasets to be experimented, and the best model performance needs to be validated along with the optimal feature extraction.

REFERENCES

Ablaza, F. I., Danganan, T. O. D., Javier, B. P. L., Manalang, K. S., Montalvo, D. E. V., & Ambata, L. U. (2014). A small vocabulary automatic filipino speech profanity suppression system using hybrid Hidden Markov Model/Artificial Neural Network (HMM/ANN) keyword spotting framework. *2014 International Conference on Humanoid, Nanotechnology, Information Technology, Communication and Control, Environment and Management (HNICEM)*, 1–5. https://doi.org/10.1109/HNICEM.2014.7016183

Alcântara, C. D. S., Feijó, D., & Moreira, V. P. (2020). Offensive video detection: Dataset and baseline results. *Proceedings of the 12th Language Resources and Evaluation Conference*, 4309–4319. https://aclanthology.org/2020.lrec-1.531

Ali, R., Farooq, U., Arshad, U., Shahzad, W., & Beg, M. O. (2022). Hate speech detection on Twitter using transfer learning. *Computer Speech & Language*, 74, 101365. https://doi.org/10.1016/J.CSL.2022.101365

Aluru, S. S., Mathew, B., Saha, P., & Mukherjee, A. (2020). Deep learning models for multilingual hate speech detection. *Social and Information Networks*, 1–16. http://arxiv.org/abs/2004.06465

Ashraf, M. (2020). Online hate speech in India: Issues and regulatory challenges. *International Journal of Law Management & Humanities*, 3(5), 919–937. https://www.vidhiaagaz.com

Ashraf, N., Rafiq, A., Butt, S., Shehzad, H. M. F., Sidorov, G., & Gelbukh, A. (2022). YouTube based religious hate speech and extremism detection dataset with machine learning baselines. *Journal of Intelligent & Fuzzy Systems*, 42(5), 4769–4777. https://doi.org/10.3233/JIFS-219264

Ayo, F. E., Folorunso, O., Ibharalu, F. T., & Osinuga, I. A. (2020). Machine learning techniques for hate speech classification of twitter data: State-of-The-Art, future challenges and research directions. *Computer Science Review*, 38, 100311. https://doi.org/10.1016/j.cosrev.2020.100311

Baevski, A., Zhou, H., Mohamed, A., & Auli, M. (2020). wav2vec 2.0: A framework for self-supervised learning of speech representations. *Advances in Neural Information Processing Systems*. https://doi.org/10.48550/arxiv.2006.11477

Bigoulaeva, I., Hangya, V., & Fraser, A. (2021). Cross-lingual transfer learning for hate speech detection. *Proceedings of the First Workshop on Language Technology for Equality, Diversity and Inclusion*, 15–25. https://aclanthology.org/2021.ltedi-1.3

Boishakhi, F. T., Shill, P. C., & Alam, M. G. R. (2021). Multi-modal hate speech detection using machine learning. *Proceedings-2021 IEEE International Conference on Big Data, Big Data 2021*, 4496–4499. https://doi.org/10.1109/BIGDATA52589.2021.9671955

Bosco, C., Sanguinetti, M., Dell'Orletta, F., Poletto, F., & Tesconi, M. (2018). Overview of the EVALITA 2018 hate speech detection task. In *EVALITA@ CLiC-it*. CEUR-WS. https://doi.org/10.4000/BOOKS.AACCADEMIA.4503

Busso, C., Bulut, M., Lee, C. C., Kazemzadeh, A., Mower, E., Kim, S., Chang, J. N., Lee, S., & Narayanan, S. S. (2008). IEMOCAP: Interactive emotional dyadic motion capture database. *Language Resources and Evaluation, 42*, 335–359. https://doi.org/10.1007/S10579-008-9076-6

Cyberbullying in Plain Sight-A McAfee Connected Family Report. (2022).

Davidson, T., Warmsley, D., Macy, M., & Weber, I. (2017). Automated hate speech detection and the problem of offensive language. *Proceedings of the 11th International Conference on Web and Social Media, ICWSM 2017, 512–515.*

Ganchev, T., Fakotakis, N., & Kokkinakis, G. (2005). Comparative evaluation of various MFCC implementations on the speaker verification task. *Proceedings of the 10th International Conference on Speech and Computer (SPECOM 2005), 191–194.*

Gangwar, A., Fidalgo, E., Alegre, E., & González-Castro, V. (2017). Pornography and child sexual abuse detection in image and video: A comparative evaluation. *Proceedings of the 8th International Conference on Imaging for Crime Detection and Prevention (ICDP 2017), 37–42.* https://doi.org/10.1049/IC.2017.0046

Genç, R. (2017). The importance of communication in sustainability & sustainable strategies. *Procedia Manufacturing, 8,* 511–516. https://doi.org/10.1016/J.PROMFG.2017.02.065

Gupta, V., Sharon, R., Sawhney, R., & Mukherjee, D. (2022). Adima: Abuse detection in multilingual audio. *Proceedings of the 2022 IEEE International Conference on Acoustics, Speech and Signal Processing (ICASSP), 6172–6176.* https://doi.org/10.1109/ICASSP43922.2022.9746718

Hershey, S., Chaudhuri, S., Ellis, D. P. W., Gemmeke, J. F., Jansen, A., Moore, R. C., Plakal, M., Platt, D., Saurous,R. A., Seybold, B., Slaney, M., Weiss, R. J., & Wilson, K. (2017). CNN architectures for large-scale audio classification. *Proceedings of the 2017 IEEE International Conference on Acoustics, Speech and Signal Processing (ICASSP), 131–135.* https://doi.org/10.1109/ICASSP.2017.7952132

Holkar, S., Sawarkar, S. D., & Vaikole, S. (2020). Audio and video toxic comments detection and classification. *International Journal of Engineering Research & Technology (IJERT), 9*(12), 162–166.

Hossain Junaid, M. I., Hossain, F., & Rahman, R. M. (2021). Bangla hate speech detection in videos using machine learning. *Proceedings of the 2021 IEEE 12th Annual Ubiquitous Computing, Electronics and Mobile Communication Conference (UEMCON), 347–351.* https://doi.org/10.1109/UEMCON53757.2021.9666550

Kiela, D., Firooz, H., Mohan, A., Goswami, V., Singh, A., Ringshia, P., & Testuggine, D. (2020). The hateful memes challenge: Detecting hate speech in multimodal memes. *Advances in Neural Information Processing Systems.* https://doi.org/10.48550/arxiv.2005.04790

Kumar, G., Singh, J. P., & Kumar, A. (2021). A deep multi-modal neural network for the identification of hate speech from social media. In *Lecture Notes in Computer Science (including subseries Lecture Notes in Artificial Intelligence and Lecture Notes in Bioinformatics): Vol. 12896 LNCS* (pp. 670–680). Springer Science and Business Media Deutschland GmbH. https://doi. org/10.1007/978-3-030-85447-8_55/COVER

Lu, Y., Cheung, Y.-M., & Tang, Y. Y. (2020). Adaptive chunk-based dynamic weighted majority for imbalanced data streams with concept drift. *IEEE Transactions on Neural Networks and Learning Systems, 31(8)*, 2764–2778. https://doi. org/10.1109/TNNLS.2019.2951814

Lynn, T., Endo, P. T., Rosati, P., Silva, I., Santos, G. L., & Ging, D. (2019). A comparison of machine learning approaches for detecting misogynistic speech in urban dictionary. *2019 International Conference on Cyber Situational Awareness, Data Analytics and Assessment, Cyber SA 2019*, 1–8. https://doi.org/10.1109/ CyberSA.2019.8899669

MacAvaney, S., Yao, H. R., Yang, E., Russell, K., Goharian, N., & Frieder, O. (2019). Hate speech detection: Challenges and solutions. *PLoS ONE, 14(8)*, e0221152. https://doi.org/10.1371/JOURNAL.PONE.0221152

Mathew, B., Saha, P., Yimam, S. M., Biemann, C., Goyal, P., & Mukherjee, A. (2020). HateXplain: A benchmark dataset for explainable hate speech detection. *35th AAAI Conference on Artificial Intelligence, AAAI 2021, 17A*, 14867–14875. https://doi.org/10.48550/arxiv.2012.10289

McFee, B., Raffel, C., Liang, D., Ellis, D. P. W., McVicar, M., Battenberg, E., & Nieto, O. (2015). Librosa: Audio and music signal analysis in Python. *Proceedings of the 14th Python in Science Conference (SCIPY 2015)*, 18–24. https://doi. org/10.25080/MAJORA-7B98E3ED-003

Mollas, I., Chrysopoulou, Z., Karlos, S., & Tsoumakas, G. (2022). ETHOS: A multi-label hate speech detection dataset. *Complex and Intelligent Systems*. https:// doi.org/10.1007/s40747-021-00608-2

Mozafari, M., Farahbakhsh, R., & Crespi, N. (2019). A BERT-based transfer learning approach for hate speech detection in online social media. In H. Cherifi, S. Gaito, J. Mendes, E. Moro, & L. Rocha (Eds.), *Complex Networks and Their Applications VIII. Complex Networks 2019, Studies in Computational Intelligence* (Vol. 881, pp. 928–940). Springer, Cham. https:// doi.org/10.1007/978-3-030-36687-2_77

Orts, Ò. G. I. (2019). Multilingual detection of hate speech against immigrants and women in Twitter at SemEval-2019 Task 5: Frequency analysis interpolation for hate in speech detection. *Proceedings of the 13th International Workshop on Semantic Evaluation*, 460–463. https://doi.org/10.18653/V1/S19–2081

Ousidhoum, N., Lin, Z., Zhang, H., Song, Y., & Yeung, D. Y. (2019). Multilingual and multi-aspect hate speech analysis. *Proceedings of the 2019 Conference on Empirical Methods in Natural Language Processing and the 9th International Joint Conference on Natural Language Processing (EMNLP-IJCNLP)*, 4675–4684. https://doi.org/10.18653/V1/D19-1474

Pan, S. J., & Yang, Q. (2010). A survey on transfer learning. *IEEE Transactions on Knowledge and Data Engineering, 22(10)*, 1345–1359. https://doi.org/10.1109/ TKDE.2009.191

Rahut, S. K., Sharmin, R., & Tabassum, R. (2020). Bengali abusive speech classification: A transfer learning approach using VGG-16. *Proceedings of the 2020 Emerging Technology in Computing, Communication and Electronics (ETCCE)*, 1–6. https://doi.org/10.1109/ETCCE51779.2020.9350919

Rana, A., & Jha, S. (2022). Emotion based hate speech detection using multimodal learning. *ArXiv*, 1–9. http://arxiv.org/abs/2202.06218

Reimers, N., & Gurevych, I. (2019). Sentence-BERT: Sentence embeddings using Siamese BERT-Networks. *Proceedings of the 2019 Conference on Empirical Methods in Natural Language Processing and the 9th International Joint Conference on Natural Language Processing (EMNLP-IJCNLP)*, 3982–3992. https://doi.org/10.18653/V1/D19-1410

Roy, P. K., Tripathy, A. K., Das, T. K., & Gao, X. Z. (2020). A framework for hate speech detection using deep convolutional neural network. *IEEE Access*, 8, 204951–204962. https://doi.org/10.1109/ACCESS.2020.3037073

Safaya, A., Abdullatif, M., & Yuret, D. (2020). KUISAIL at SemEval-2020 Task 12: BERT-CNN for offensive speech identification in social media. *Proceedings of the Fourteenth Workshop on Semantic Evaluation*, 2054–2059. https://doi.org/10.18653/V1/2020.SEMEVAL-1.271

Sharon, R., Shah, H., Mukherjee, D., & Gupta, V. (2022). Multilingual and multimodal abuse detection. *ArXiv Preprint ArXiv ....* https://arxiv.org/abs/2204.02263

Sutejo, T. L., & Lestari, D. P. (2019). Indonesia hate speech detection using deep learning. *Proceedings of the 2018 International Conference on Asian Language Processing, IALP 2018*, 39–43. https://doi.org/10.1109/IALP.2018.8629154

The State of Online Harassment. (n.d.). Pew Research Center. Retrieved October 1, 2022, from https://www.pewresearch.org/internet/2021/01/13/the-state-of-online-harassment/

Touahri, I., & Mazroui, A. (2022). Offensive language and hate speech detection based on transfer learning. *Advanced Intelligent Systems for Sustainable Development (AI2SD'2020), AI2SD 2020, Advances in Intelligent Systems and Computing*, 1418, 300–311. https://doi.org/10.1007/978-3-030-90639-9_24

Wiedemann, G., Yimam, S. M., & Biemann, C. (2020). UHH-LT at SemEval-2020 Task 12: Fine-tuning of pre-trained transformer networks for offensive language detection. *Proceedings of the 14th International Workshops on Semantic Evaluation, SemEval 2020*, 1638–1644. https://doi.org/10.18653/V1/2020.SEMEVAL-1.213

Wu, C. S., & Bhandary, U. (2020). Detection of hate speech in videos using machine learning. *Proceedings of the 2020 International Conference on Computational Science and Computational Intelligence, CSCI 2020*, 585–590. https://doi.org/10.1109/CSCI51800.2020.00104

Yousefi, M., & Emmanouilidou, D. (2021). Audio-based toxic language classification using self-attentive convolutional neural network. *Proceedings of the 2021 29th European Signal Processing Conference (EUSIPCO)*, 11–15. https://doi.org/10.23919/EUSIPCO54536.2021.9616001

Chapter 4

A comprehensive review of toxicity analysis using deep learning techniques

Pranav Kulkarni and Ishan G. Gala
Marathwada Mitramandal's College of Engineering

CONTENTS

4.1 Introduction   49
4.2 Methodology   50
    4.2.1 Data preprocessing   51
        4.2.1.1 Preprocessing for transformer-based models   51
        4.2.1.2 Preprocessing for recurrent neural networks   51
    4.2.2 Model architectures and training process   51
        4.2.2.1 Transformer-based models   51
        4.2.2.2 Recurrent neural network model   53
        4.2.2.3 Training process   54
4.3 Results   55
4.4 Conclusions and future directions   57
References   57

4.1 INTRODUCTION

Sentiment analysis, also known as opinion mining or emotion artificial intelligence (AI), is contextual text mining that identifies and extracts subjective information from sources. It helps companies understand how the public feels about their brand, product, or service while monitoring online conversations. Recent developments in deep learning have greatly increased algorithms' capacity for text analysis. The inventive application of cutting-edge AI methods can be a useful instrument for doing an in-depth study.

Text mining technologies must handle a lot of document operations quickly and correctly in order to handle this volume of data. Text classification is a fundamental component of many applications, including subject categorization, sentiment analysis, information filtering, online searching, and natural language processing (NLP) in general.

The text produced by an interactive online communication conceals a number of risks, including toxicity, online bullying, and fake news. A statement that is toxic is one that is likely to cause someone to quit a debate, regardless of whether it involves physical or verbal violence. Online harassment, bullying, and personal attacks can all be categorized as toxic

DOI: 10.1201/9781003107767-4

comments. Unfortunately, it is a common occurrence in the online world and produces a variety of issues. The risk is elevated by the growth of social media platforms and the expansion of online communication.

Although there are attempts to make online environments safer using crowdsourcing voting systems or the ability to reject a comment, these methods are typically ineffective and fail to foresee potential toxicity.

It is crucial to automatically identify and predict poisonous comments in real time because doing so would help internet users avoid a number of negative consequences. For achieving the same, a methodology that combines crowdsourcing and machine learning to analyze personal attacks at scale was proposed by Wulczyn et al. (2017) in this direction, which used logistic regression and multilayer perceptrons.

Various approaches have been applied before to this problem, and Georgakopoulos et al. (2018) used convolutional neural networks (CNNs) for the classification of toxic comments, in which they added an embedding layer prior to the convolutional and pooling layers for the conversion of text data into vector form, which was followed by a feed-forward layer at the end for the purpose of outputting the class. Zhang and Luo (2019) showed the effectiveness of neural network approaches for the classification of toxic comments. van Aken et al. (2018) put forth the challenges for toxic comment classification along with building upon the CNN and bidirectional long short-term memory network (Bi-LSTM) approach. Related research also includes the investigation of hate speech, as shown in Burnap and Williams (2016), Davidson et al. (2017), and Schmidt and Wiegand (2017).

Building on similar lines, in this work, we employ the Wikipedia toxicity dataset as built and used by Wulczyn et al. (2017) with additional multilingual modifications in an attempt to provide a comprehensive review of the performance of contemporary recurrent neural network (RNN) along with the models based on the self-attention-based transformer architecture.

The rest of the chapter is organized as follows: In Section 4.2, we present the methodology that has been used along with the model architectures and descriptions.

In Section 4.3, we provide the results along with the comparative analysis of the models used. Section 4.4 is devoted to the provision of our conclusions.

Section 4.5 contains all the references used for this work.

4.2 METHODOLOGY

The methodology followed in this chapter includes data preprocessing and applying the specified deep learning models to the dataset. The comments in this configuration for Wikipedia-toxicity-multilingual come from a collection of non-English Wikipedia talk page comments that Jigsaw has evaluated for toxicity. Each comment has a binary value (0 or 1) that indicates whether the majority of annotators have rated it as poisonous or not. This configuration's comments are available in a variety of languages (Turkish, Italian, Spanish, Portuguese, Russian, and French).

4.2.1 Data preprocessing

The preprocessing of the data has to be done in two different ways, as the input format required for the transformer-based models is quite different when compared to that of the format required for RNNs.

4.2.1.1 Preprocessing for transformer-based models

The preprocessing of data is independent for each of the models, wherein the respective tokenizers of the said model are used to encode the data in batches, which mainly include three operations:

a. Addition of attention masks.
b. Create token-type IDs.
c. Padding to maximum length.

After the encoding of the data, a data pipeline is created for efficient training, using the tf.data pipelining techniques specified in the TensorFlow core module that includes splitting of the dataset into two parts, namely, training set and validation set.

4.2.1.2 Preprocessing for recurrent neural networks

The preprocessing steps are pretty simple for RNNs when compared to those of transformer-based models.

The complete text corpus is vectorized using the TextVectorization layer from Keras' preprocessing module inside the model; hence, no additional preprocessing is required apart from the removal of unused characters and special characters that add no meaning to the sentence. Further steps also include splitting of the dataset into two parts, namely, the training set and the validation set to ensure that the model does not overfit.

4.2.2 Model architectures and training process

This work includes the application of four different transformer-based models and an RNN approach; the architectures of which are as follows:

4.2.2.1 Transformer-based models

4.2.2.1.1 BERT base

BERT (Bidirectional Encoder Representations from Transformers) is a language model introduced by Devlin et al. (2018). In order to aid computers in

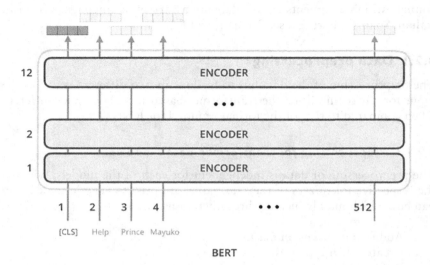

Figure 4.1 BERT architecture. (Image Credits: http://jalammar.github.io/illustrated-bert/.)

deciphering the meaning of ambiguous words in text, BERT makes advantage of the surrounding text to offer context. The BERT framework may be modified after being pretrained on Wikipedia text using question-and-answer datasets.

BERT is built on transformers, a deep learning model, where the weights between the input and output elements are dynamically set based on their connection (Figure 4.1).

4.2.2.1.2 DistilBERT base

DistilBERT is a BERT-based transformer model introduced by Sanh et al. (2019) that is compact, quick, affordable, and light. In order to shrink a BERT model by 40% during the pretraining stage, knowledge distillation is used. The authors propose a triple loss to exploit the inductive biases that larger models acquire during pretraining, combining language modeling, distillation, and cosine-distance losses (Figure 4.2).

4.2.2.1.3 RoBERTa base

The RoBERTa model was presented in RoBERTa: A Robustly Optimized BERT Pretraining Approach by Liu et al. (2019). It is based on Google's 2018 BERT model.

It improves on BERT by removing the next-sentence pretraining target, training with noticeably larger mini-batches, and altering crucial hyperparameters.

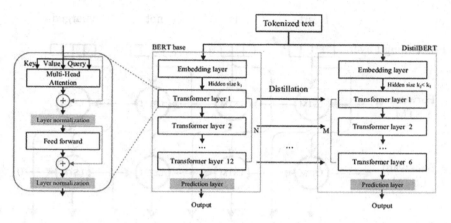

Figure 4.2 DistilBERT architecture. (Image Credits: Dahou et al. 2022.)

RoBERTa also changes the masking pattern dynamically. To avoid utilizing a single static mask, training data are copied and masked ten times in BERT, each time using a different masking approach throughout 40 epochs. As a result, the same mask is used for four epochs. This tactic is contrasted with dynamic masking, where a new mask is created each time an input is passed into the model.

4.2.2.1.4 ALBERT base

ALBERT is a transformer architecture built on the BERT platform but with significantly less parameters as put forth by Lan et al. (2019). Two parameter-reduction strategies are used to achieve this. An embedding parameterization with factors is the first. By dividing the enormous vocabulary-embedding matrix into two smaller matrices, the size of the hidden layers and the size of vocabulary embedding are separated. This makes it simpler to raise the hidden size without considerably expanding the vocabulary embeddings' parameter size. Parameter sharing between layers is the second method. The parameter would not increase along with the network's depth thanks to this method.

For the purpose of predicting sentence order, ALBERT also uses a self-supervised loss. The main focus of sentence order prediction (SOP) is on inter-sentence coherence, and it was created to overcome the shortcomings of the next-sentence prediction loss that was suggested in the original BERT.

4.2.2.2 Recurrent neural network model

This manuscript includes the usage of an enhanced RNN, or sequential network, called an LSTM put forth by Hochreiter and Schmidhuber (1996),

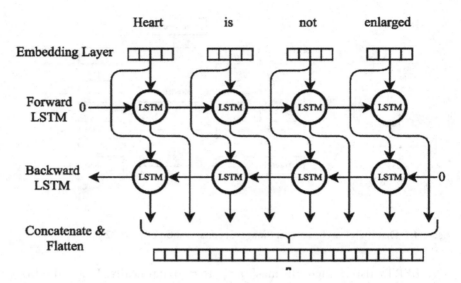

Figure 4.3 Bidirectional LSTM architecture. (Image Credits: https://paperswithcode. com/method/bilstm.)

which permits information to endure. It can fix the vanishing gradient problem with the RNN. RNNs, often known as RNNs, are used for permanent memory.

In a bidirectional LSTM, the input flows in two directions, making a Bi-LSTM different from the regular LSTM. With the regular LSTM, the input flow is unidirectional. To preserve both the past and the future, Bi-LSTM allows the input to flow in both directions (Figure 4.3).

4.2.2.3 Training process

The training of all the transformer-based models was done on tensor processing units (TPUs) as provided by Kaggle for the reduction of training time and easier pipelining.

In the preprocessing stage, the dataset was converted into an input pipeline that made the use of tf.data API and Google Cloud Storage buckets, as TPUs require continuous data streaming from Cloud Storage Buckets for the purpose of training.

Due to the extremely large size and high computational complexity of the transformer-based models, training them for even small amounts of time provides with accurate results; hence, in this case, each of the four models was trained for two epochs/iterations. After the training process was complete, the models were evaluated on the validation set and the metrics were noted accordingly for comparison.

For the Bi-LSTM model, the data were vectorized using the TextVectorization layer from Keras along with an embedding layer in the pipeline, and then the hyperparameters for the model were derived using the Keras-Tuner utility. Further, the model was trained on GPU for 20 epochs/iterations with an early stopping mechanism, since LSTM models are not as compute-heavy as transformer-based models.

For both types of models, the optimizer used for training purposes was Adam (Kingma and Ba, 2015) with empirically derived specific learning rates for different models.

4.3 RESULTS

For the evaluation of the models on the validation dataset, the following metrics were considered:

1. *Accuracy.* The accuracy of the model under testing was obtained by running it on the validation data in the dataset, and that validation accuracy was considered for comparison.
2. *Loss.* The loss function is another metric that was considered for the evaluation of the models. Since the problem statement was that of binary classification (either toxic or nontoxic), the loss function used while compiling the models was binary cross-entropy/log loss.

The comparative analysis of the models is given below (see Table 4.1 and Figures 4.4–4.6).

Figures 4.4 and 4.5 give a visual insight into the metrics applied for the evaluation of the models. Since the RNN was trained for a larger number of iterations, its accuracy over time is as follows (Figure 4.6).

From the metrics, it is evident that the Bi-LSTM model seems to perform better than the transformer-based models; however, upon looking at the loss values of each model, it is clear that the loss of the RNN is greater than that of BERT, which implies that the RNN is prone to making big errors in prediction, albeit lesser times. This leads to the implication that the RNN model is possibly overfitting on the data, thus providing high numbers of accuracy, when in reality it may not be able to generalize well on external data. Table 4.1 shows accuracy and loss values of models.

Table 4.1 Accuracy and loss values of models

Model	Accuracy (%)	Loss
Bi-LSTM	88.27	0.3983
BERT base	87.82	0.3028
DistilBERT base	86.98	0.3305
RoBERTa base	84.97	0.3884
ALBERT base	84.62	0.4307

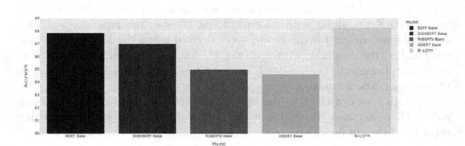

Figure 4.4 Bar plot of accuracy.

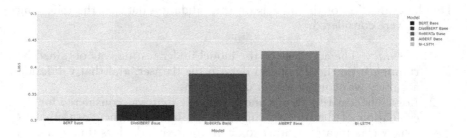

Figure 4.5 Bar plot of loss.

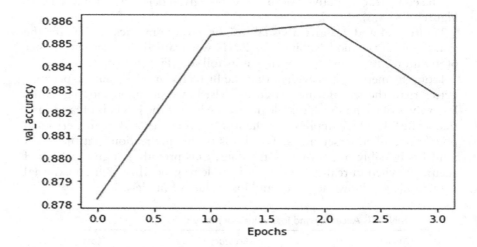

Figure 4.6 RNN model accuracy vs. iterations.

On the other hand, BERT provides high accuracy as well as low loss numbers, which indicates that a transformer-based model is able to generalize better on the data as it is sequential data.

Variations of BERT provide lesser accuracy numbers due to different pre-training techniques used in the backbone of the model as well as modified architectures.

4.4 CONCLUSIONS AND FUTURE DIRECTIONS

Large-language models are all the more famous right now, and currently, transformer-based models are outperforming all contemporary techniques on natural language processing tasks including semantic classification, sentiment analysis, next-sentence prediction, and text summarization.

In the current work, the same transformer-based models are used along with a contemporary RNN model for toxicity analysis and classification. The results show that while the RNN gives a higher accuracy, it also outputs higher loss values. On the other hand, BERT provides equally comparable accuracy values with less loss; thus, it can be inferred that transformer-based models are able to generalize better on natural language tasks.

Further work that the authors intend to undertake is to train the larger variants of transformer-based models for higher number of iterations on larger datasets to see how they perform on big data, a phenomenon that has taken the world by storm in the current times.

REFERENCES

Burnap, P., & Williams, M. L. (2016). Us and them: Identifying cyber hate on Twitter across multiple protected characteristics. *EPJ Data Science, 5*, 1–15.

Dahou, A., Mabrouk, A., Elsayed Abd Elaziz, M., Kayed, M., El-Henawy, I., Alshathri, S., & Ali, A. (2022). Improving crisis events detection using DistilBERT with hunger games search algorithm. *Mathematics, 10*, 447. doi: 10.3390/math10030447

Davidson, T., Warmsley, D., Macy, M., & Weber, I. (2017, May). Automated hate speech detection and the problem of offensive language. In *Proceedings of the International AAAI Conference on Web and Social Media* (Vol. 11, No. 1, pp. 512–515).

Devlin, J., Chang, M. W., Lee, K., & Toutanova, K. (2018). Bert: Pre-training of deep bidirectional transformers for language understanding. *arXiv preprint arXiv:1810.04805.*

Georgakopoulos, S. V., Tasoulis, S. K., Vrahatis, A. G., & Plagianakos, V. P. (2018, July). Convolutional neural networks for toxic comment classification. In *Proceedings of the 10th Hellenic Conference on Artificial Intelligence* (pp. 1–6).

Hochreiter, S., & Schmidhuber, J. (1997). Long short-term memory. *Neural Computation, 9*, 1735–80. doi: 10.1162/neco.1997.9.8.1735

Kingma, D., & Ba, J. (2014). Adam: A method for stochastic optimization. International Conference on Learning Representations.

Lan, Z., Chen, M., Goodman, S., Gimpel, K., Sharma, P., & Soricut, R. (2019). Albert: A lite bert for self-supervised learning of language representations. *arXiv preprint arXiv:1909.11942*.

Liu, Y., Ott, M., Goyal, N., Du, J., Joshi, M., Chen, D., … & Stoyanov, V. (2019). Roberta: A robustly optimized bert pretraining approach. *arXiv preprint arXiv:1907.11692*.

Sanh, V., Debut, L., Chaumond, J., & Wolf, T. (2019). DistilBERT, a distilled version of BERT: Smaller, faster, cheaper and lighter. *arXiv preprint arXiv:1910.01108*.

Schmidt, A., & Wiegand, M. (2017, April). A survey on hate speech detection using natural language processing. In *Proceedings of the Fifth International Workshop on Natural Language Processing for Social Media* (pp. 1–10).

Van Aken, B., Risch, J., Krestel, R., & Löser, A. (2018). Challenges for toxic comment classification: An in-depth error analysis. *arXiv preprint arXiv:1809.07572*.

Wulczyn, E., Thain, N., & Dixon, L. (2017, April). Ex machina: Personal attacks seen at scale. In *Proceedings of the 26th International Conference on World Wide Web* (pp. 1391–1399).

Zhang, Z., & Luo, L. (2019). Hate speech detection: A solved problem? the challenging case of long tail on twitter. *Semantic Web*, *10*(5), 925–945.

Chapter 5

Literature review on zero-knowledge proof and its applications

Priya A. Sirsat

All India Shri Shivaji Memorial Society's
Institute of Information Technology

Aayush P. Khandekar

Vishwakarma Institute of Technology

CONTENTS

5.1 Introduction   59
5.2 Zero-knowledge proof   60
    5.2.1 Interactive zero-knowledge proof   61
    5.2.2 Noninteractive zero-knowledge proof   62
5.3 Bibliometrics analyses   63
5.4 Literature review   63
    5.4.1 Zcash coin   63
    5.4.2 zk-SNARKs   64
    5.4.3 zk-STARKs   64
    5.4.4 Additional examples   65
5.5 Conclusion and future direction   65
References   66

5.1 INTRODUCTION

The twenty-first century has witnessed some global changes in all sectors due to the rise of the Internet. The world of digitalization has documented the growth of computers from making basic mathematical calculations, to developing algorithms that are capable of solving complex problems. Digitalization and the Internet in today's era have changed people's lifestyles by expanding business opportunities and social networks. Knowingly or unknowingly, every human is always within a reachable range of a technological product, be it a cell phone or a computer. Programming automation has made it easier to automate not only complex tasks but also repetitive tasks. Cyber security is one such task. The world has adapted to this automation that we rely on its security and integrity due to its efficiency (Tarter 2017). Due to this dependence on the automation of cyber security, cybercriminals abuse the privacy of individuals or businesses and

DOI: 10.1201/9781003107767-5

59

exploit the system to obtain sensitive information. Most business transactions, commercial transactions, personal information, human interests, and emotions take place on the Internet. Cybersecurity is one of the fastest growing technological areas not only in the IT sector but also in healthcare, banking, education, military, government, and public sector. While this is an excellent development in terms of digitalization, it is also a golden ticket for cybercriminals.

The exponential rise in the number of cyber-attacks has made cybersecurity a billion-dollar industry. Cybercrime accounts for 1 trillion US dollars, which is significantly higher than the amount predicted in 2018. It also accounts for more than 1% of the global gross domestic product (GDP). An increase in data breaches provides nourishment for the statistical growth of this industry. The average cost of a data breach increased from $3.86 million to $4.24 million from 2020 to 2021 (Rid and Buchanan 2015). One of the prominent cyber breaches took place in April 2021. The data of more than half a billion Facebook users was leaked online free of cost. The data of the users contained personal information such as their name, phone number, Facebook ID, location, birth date, and bio description. This data collectively belonged to over 100 countries, with over 30 million records from the United States, 11 million from the United Kingdom, and 6 million from India. In this data breach, cybercriminals took advantage of the fact that the users were able to find others through phone numbers. Such incidents make the crowd question the security of their data on social media platforms. To overcome such situations, one possible solution could be to not provide personal details in the first place. The methodology that enables us to objectively assess a significant number of scientific papers is bibliometrics or bibliometric analysis. As a result, it enables trend analysis and statistical data analysis within its specialized fields. In conclusion, Zero-Knowledge Range Proof (ZKRP) enables the demonstration of the interval to which a secret integer belongs. If we define this range as all numbers between 18 and 200, for instance, a person can demonstrate her adult status by using the ZKRP program. This grants her permission to use a specific service without disclosing her exact age in accordance with any legislation. In the context of payment systems, it is feasible to use ZKRP to demonstrate that the amount of money being transferred from party A to party B is positive; otherwise, if the amount is negative, such a transaction would actually send money from B to A.

5.2 ZERO-KNOWLEDGE PROOF

A notion introduced by Goldwasser, Micali, and Rackoff (Goldreich and Oren 1994) called zero-knowledge proof (ZKP) revolves around the idea of proving the authenticity of a given statement without providing any additional information other than the statement that needs to be proven. The prover faces the challenge of proving the statement to the verifier without revealing the information that they already possess about the given statement. The verifier, on the other hand, must be able to verify that the prover is indeed providing the truth. The crucial aspects of the ZKP can be interactive and noninteractive models. Interactive verification input is mandatory for protocols implementing ZKP. Common interactive information takes the form of one or more tasks that persuade the prover to respond if the explanation is true, i.e., if the prover has requested information. If not, the verifiers can record and replay the protocol executions to convince someone that you have confidential data. Assumptions by the new party are justified because the prover has data (including that the protocol was not proven without knowing it was leaked) or because the claim was misleading. The two models, namely, interactive and noninteractive have been discussed below:

5.2.1 Interactive zero-knowledge proof

Interactive ZKPs require live interaction between verifiers and provers. The Fiat–Shamir heuristic is an interactive proof-of-knowledge technique based on creating a digital signature. This allows them to be publicly verified without the need to prove that "witnesses" or facts are always online (Rackoff and Simon 1991).

The following are the issues that can be encountered with interactive ZKPs:

I. On the other side, problems associated with this include, portability limitations—the user might need to go through the same process again to reprove the identical proof to a different validator. It could require a lot of time and effort.

II. *Unscalable.* It is complicated to use interactive ZKP since it requires both the verifier as well as the prover to be online at the same time, making the whole process cumbersome.

A few instances where interactive ZKP has been used are as follows:

I. A useful technique was shown in 2016 by the Princeton Plasma Physics Laboratory and Princeton University, namely, Nuclear Disarmament. In this technique, inspectors may determine if a piece of equipment is a nuclear weapon without having to record, share, or reveal any potentially sensitive internal processes.

II. Another useful application of interactive ZKP is when users have the ability to utilize this to validate passwords without disclosing them to the system called authenticators. Since the majority of ZKP's protocols demand bigger arbitrary inputs, a zero-knowledge password proof is a unique kind of ZKP that resolves passwords of limited length.

5.2.2 Noninteractive zero-knowledge proof

Previously, ZKP verification systems were interactive. As discussed earlier the "prover" of the information and "verifiers" had to be online at the same time to successfully perform the particular operation, this made the whole process obscure and unscalable. In 1986, Fiat and Shamir invented the Fiat–Shamir heuristic, changing interactive ZKPs to noninteractive ZKPs and modifying the drawbacks of interactive ZKPs (Santis et al. 1987).

With these modifications, the following issues with interactive ZKP were resolved:

 I. *Transferable Evidence.* Once a prover establishes a witness's evidence as true, the evidence may be published, and the subsequent prover does not need to go through the same procedure.
 II. *Scalability.* Due to modifications made to the noninteractive ZKP, which address the issue with interactive ZKPs where the prover and verifier must both be online at the same time, users no longer need to be simultaneously online.

The applications of noninteractive ZKP have been demonstrated in the following examples:

 I. Blockchain is the major application of noninteractive ZKP, and even though the sender, receiver, and transaction details remain anonymous, blockchain can be used to authenticate transactions on public blockchains.
 II. Bulletproofs were made available in 2017, as the foundation for other protocols, which are an important addition to the application of the noninteractive ZKP (Figure 5.1).

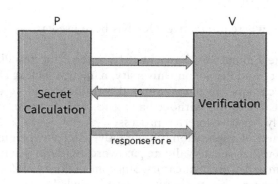

Figure 5.1 The general process of zero-knowledge proof protocol.

5.3 BIBLIOMETRICS ANALYSES

The current study examines the link between "various applications of ZKP" and authentication using bibliometrics from the methodology standpoint of a data-based analysis. Each cited item is evaluated in detail throughout the text, and each mentioned item is evaluated in depth, providing an overview and an introduction to the information gleaned from the study. Nevertheless, these data make it possible for the next works to examine the data sources succinctly and to extrapolate further statistical analysis from them in order to meet the demands of the proposed works. The data sources are then examined.

The next section, i.e., Section 5.4, discusses the real-world applications of ZKPs.

5.4 LITERATURE REVIEW

5.4.1 Zcash coin

With the aim of providing enhanced privacy to its users, Zcash was conceived by a group of well-known scientists from some of the top universities like MIT, John Hopkins, etc. Zcash is a cryptocurrency that is based on Bitcoin's codebase and they both have the same number of coins available i.e. 21 million coins in the cryptocurrency market. Though Zcash has some similarities to Bitcoin, the major differences lie in the security that they provide (Kappos et al. 2018). To ensure the privacy and security of the user data, Zcash offers its users the following two options. With the first option, the users can select the normal transaction option, which is similar to other cryptocurrencies. This option displays the full transaction history and the holdings publicly and is posted on a public blockchain. The second option provided by Zcash can be called the "shielded" option. In this option, the user can use confidential transactions and financial privacy through shielded addresses, and hence Zcash provides a strong privacy guarantee since these transactions can be fully encrypted on the blockchain. Zcash delivers this through the concept of zero knowledge (Zhang et al. 2019). Zero-Knowledge Succinct Non-Interactive Argument of Knowledge or simply zk-SNARKs are a type of cryptographic proof technology. In the first zero-knowledge protocols, there were multiple instances of communication happening back and forth between the prover and the verifier, but on the contrary, in the noninteractive zero-knowledge protocols, the prover sends only one singular piece of information to the verifier. Generating an initial setup phase as well as a common reference string which was shared with both the prover and the verifier was the most effective way to produce ZKPs that were noninteractive. The only problem that could arise was the possibility of the common reference string falling into the hands of a cyber attacker.

5.4.2 zk-SNARKs

In Bitcoin transactions, the transactions are normally validated with the help of the following set of information of the sender and the receiver, the sender address, the receiver address, and the input and output values which are displayed on the public blockchain. As zk-SNARKs use zero knowledge, it needs to prove the authenticity of the transaction between the sender and the receiver without revealing any crucial information such as the transaction amount or other details of the users. Hence, the sender of the shielded transactions creates proof to prove authenticity and a high probability that the input values sum to the output values which were received by the receiver. The sender also proves that they have the authority to spend based on the fact that they possess the private spending keys of the input notes (Pinto 2020). In Zcash, the shielded unspent transaction outputs are named commitments. These commitments are used to determine what transactions are spendable by the users. Whenever the user spends this commitment, a certain nullifier is revealed. Such commitments are nullifiers that are stored in the form of hashes to avoid disclosure of any information. These commitments are hashed with the receiver's address, the amount which was sent, a certain number rho, and a nonce r. These parameters are used to hash the commitment. These commitments are published whenever a note is created by the shielded payment. Similarly, the nullifier is hashed with the spending key and rho. The spending key is the hash of the private unique number rho from an existing commitment that has not been already spent. This provides an implication with the help of ZKP that the spender is allowed to spend.

5.4.3 zk-STARKs

One of the two transparent and scalable privacy-enhancing techniques is zk-STARKs. There is no requirement for a trusted setup because the randomness used by the verifier is publicly accessible. Zk-STARK, a kind of cryptographic proof technology, stands for Zero-Knowledge Scalable Transparent Argument of Knowledge. ZKPs, or zk-STARKs, allow users to exchange validated data or carry out computations with a third party without the other party knowing the data or results of the analysis. Before the development of zk-STARKs, zk-SNARKs were used to construct zk-proof systems, which eliminated the vulnerability of those trusted parties endangering the system's privacy since they had to initially set up the zk-proof system. In order to improve this technology, zk-STARKs distance themselves from the necessity of a stable setup. Additionally, STARKs help with the scalability and privacy problems of permissionless blockchains. Scalability is the main focus of the current zk-STARK research being performed by STARK technology pioneer StarkWare Industries, with privacy being addressed subsequently (Panait and Olimid 2020). STARKs improve scalability by allowing developers to move computations and storage off-chain. Off-chain services can generate STARK proofs that confirm the precision of off-chain calculations. These proofs are then reposted on the chain for anyone who is interested to check the calculation.

5.4.4 Additional examples

I. *Authentication Systems*. This is one of the key ideas that ZKP embraced. For the study on ZKPs, authentication techniques were utilized. In these proofs, a party wants to prove its identity to a second party using certain secret information, such as a password but does not want the second party to know anything about this secret. To use in ZKP systems, a password is often just any random number (Hasan 2019). A password proof with zero knowledge is indeed a sort of certificate of knowledge that describes the restricted size of passwords. An alternative to public key cryptography authentication techniques is provided by the zero-knowledge authentication protocols. It is especially suitable for usage in microprocessors for smart cards that have severely constrained processing power and storage space because of its low processing and memory consumption.

II. *Virtuous Behavior*. Promoting sincere activity while protecting anonymity inside cryptographic systems is one of the purposes of honest evidence or proof. The idea is to essentially require a user to employ null knowledge evidence to show that his action is proper and in compliance with the Protocol (Hasan 2019). We know that the user must act honestly in order to be able to offer a piece of legitimate evidence because of soundness. We know that the user does not violate the privacy of its secrets in the process of submitting the proof since we have no prior information.

5.5 CONCLUSION AND FUTURE DIRECTION

In conclusion, the evidence of ZKP is of vital theoretical and practical relevance to both mathematicians and cryptographers. From this, we may discover the behavior of a ZKP on certain protocols. On the other hand, we have described its applicability using instances from actual life. These days, most blockchain technologies use ZKP approaches to ensure that transactions between two parties are secure and genuine. Additionally, the ZKP is a more advanced and promising study area for distributed ledger systems and blockchain technology. Even though there are now a number of issues, such as security, scalability, and efficiency, we will witness several advances and research in this area in the following years, such as zk-STARKs, and we will finally experience an increasing number of apps using this new sort of safe digital privacy knowledge-free technology. Future research will concentrate on expanding the applicability of ZKP theory and utilizing it to tackle new issues. The calculation of mathematical formulas and the specifics of the proving technique are not explained in detail in this work for many applications, nor is the complexity of communication and computing taken into account yet. All of those will make up for our upcoming duty.

REFERENCES

Goldreich, O. and Oren, Y., 1994. Definitions and properties of zero-knowledge proof systems. *Journal of Cryptology*, 7(1), pp. 1–32.

Hasan, J., 2019. Overview and applications of zero-knowledge proof (ZKP). Nanjing: Nanjing University of Posts and Telecommunications.

Kappos, G., Yousaf, H., Maller, M. and Meiklejohn, S., 2018. An empirical analysis of anonymity in zcash. In *27th USENIX Security Symposium (USENIX Security 18)* (pp. 463–477).

Panait, A.E. and Olimid, R.F., 2020, November. On using zk-SNARKs and zk-STARKs in blockchain-based identity management. In *International Conference on Information Technology and Communications Security* (pp. 130–145). Springer, Cham.

Pinto, A.M., 2020. An introduction to the use of zk-SNARKs in blockchains. In *Mathematical Research for Blockchain Economy* (pp. 233–249). Springer, Cham.

Rackoff, C. and Simon, D.R., 1991, August. Non-interactive zero-knowledge proof of knowledge and chosen ciphertext attack. In *Annual International Cryptology Conference* (pp. 433–444). Springer, Berlin, Heidelberg.

Rid, T. and Buchanan, B., 2015. Attributing cyber attacks. *Journal of Strategic Studies*, *38*(1–2), pp. 4–37.

Santis, A.D., Micali, S. and Persiano, G., 1987, August. Non-interactive zero-knowledge proof systems. In *Conference on the Theory and Application of Cryptographic Techniques* (pp. 52–72). Springer, Berlin, Heidelberg.

Tarter, A., 2017. Importance of cyber security. In *Community policing-A European Perspective* (pp. 213–230). Springer, Cham.

Zhang, R., Xue, R. and Liu, L., 2019. Security and privacy on blockchain. *ACM Computing Surveys (CSUR)*, *52*(3), pp. 1–34.

Chapter 6

Machine learning-based algorithmic comparison for fake news identification

Anuradha Yenkikar and Kavita Sultanpure
Pune Institute of Computer Technology

Manish Bali
Presidency University

CONTENTS

6.1	Introduction	68
6.2	Related work	69
6.3	Algorithms	71
	6.3.1 Naive Bayes	71
	6.3.2 Support vector machine	72
	6.3.3 Random forest	72
	6.3.4 Decision trees	72
	6.3.5 Logistic regression	72
	6.3.6 Passive aggressive algorithm	73
6.4	Methodology	73
	6.4.1 Data preparation	73
	6.4.1.1 Tokenization	74
	6.4.1.2 Stop word removal	74
	6.4.1.3 Stemming	74
	6.4.2 TF–IDF	75
	6.4.3 Classification	76
	6.4.4 Prediction	76
	6.4.4.1 Model evaluation	76
6.5	Results	77
	6.5.1 Discussion	80
	6.5.1.1 Intra-model comparison	80
	6.5.1.2 Inter-model comparison	81
6.6	Conclusion	81
	References	82

DOI: 10.1201/9781003107767-6

6.1 INTRODUCTION

The emergence of social media has democratized content creation and has made it simple for anybody to create and disseminate knowledge on the internet. As a result, citizen journalism has emerged, allowing for significantly faster information disposal than was previously possible with newspapers, radio, and television. Taking away the traditional media's gatekeeping role has left the public open to the spread of misinformation, which can now travel at breakneck speed across the same democratic path. This has resulted in the dissemination of false information, which is often manufactured either to increase network traffic and profit financially from the presentation of online advertisements such as clickbait, or to influence individual people's beliefs, and ultimately to influence important events such as elections.

There is ample proof that enormous amounts of fake information were used during the 2016 US presidential election [1]. Naturally, social media sites like Facebook and Twitter place a high priority on reducing the dissemination of false information. Fact-checking organizations like Snopes, Factcheck, and PolitiFact, which manually verify allegations, have led additional efforts to battle fake news. Unfortunately, for a variety of reasons, this is insufficient. First, manual fact checking is time consuming, and debunking erroneous information occurs far too late to make an influence. Also, automatic fact checking falls behind in terms of accuracy, and users generally do not trust it. Debunking, especially when done by credible fact-checking organizations, is ineffective in persuading individuals who already believe in incorrect information. A third, and possibly more promising technique for combating fake news is to focus on its source. Even though fake news is largely spread through social media, it still needs a 'home', or a place to be published. As a result, if a website has published incorrect information in the past, it is likely to do so again. One of the most basic strategies used by journalists in traditional media to verify information is determining the dependability of the source. Our system detects fake news present in the data spread on the social network such as Facebook, Twitter, and other resources. Various machine learning algorithms are used to find such types of fake news and benchmarks. They are chosen as fake news can be easily and automatically detected using ML algorithms as seen from literature. Also, their accuracy is good, and they are easy to implement.

The key contributions from this study are as follows:

- Benchmark study of different textual properties using various machine learning algorithms that makeup news articles which can be generalized to achieve optimum results when exposed to any domain.
- Comparison of the best performing models developed based on existing approaches.

The content of the chapter has been divided into the following sections: Section 6.2 defines related work, i.e., the basic evaluation of the existing research that have been reviewed, wherein all the methods used in these chapters have been discussed. In Section 6.3, we describe the algorithms used in this comparative study that gave the best results from the existing research reviewed followed by the methodology adopted in Section 6.4. Results of different algorithms with respect to accuracy, precision, recall, and F1-score are compared and discussed in Section 6.5. Section 6.6 outlines the conclusion and future work followed by references at the end.

6.2 RELATED WORK

In social sciences, research on fake news reporting has been studied for a very long time, since the 1950s. Williams' primary definition of fake news states that it must be persistent as well as intentional, i.e., represent a conscious act or choice and demonstrate a systematic trend rather than an isolated incident. As a result, the focus of this chapter is on purposeful fake news, which is used by journalists and other stakeholders to achieve a specific goal. This distinction is made to clarify on the false news we are discussing and other forms of unintended fake news in the press. The impact of news values on production of news, as well as subsequent consumption of news by readers from various backgrounds, are both sources of unintentional false information. The consequences of a topic's general visibility or societal importance, or the proximity of a noteworthy event to the location of the news producer and audience, are a few examples of news values. Using a Gullible Bayes classifier, authors in reference [2] proposed a straightforward approach for detecting fake news. They memorized practically everything from BuzzFeed News and put the Naive Bayes classifier to test. Within the test set, the dataset was derived from Facebook news and achieved 74% precision. Authors in reference [3] developed a system for finding Fake News on Twitter using a robot. This method was linked to Twitter, according to the researchers. Furthermore, rather than hiring writers, using nonprofessional swarm sources could be a more efficient and cost-effective way to quickly categorize true and false memes.

In reference [4], a feature was implemented into a chatbot for FB messenger and validated, which resulted in detecting fake news with an accuracy of 81.7%. In reference [5], researchers shared insights, innovative methodologies, and theories from other domains by carrying out a multidisciplinary literature study. In reference [6], authors utilize a machine learning approach to recommend a solution for the fake news recognizable proof issue. This research investigates distinctive literary qualities that can be utilized to contrast between wrong and genuine substance. They work on a combination of a few machine learning algorithms using approaches around those properties, which are not well explored in literature. Before elections, authors in references [7,8] investigated the economics of fake news and provided fresh statistics on its consumption utilizing information about online activity, fact-checking website archives, and the outcomes of a recent online survey. In reference [9], data is collected using a variety of methods, and data mining techniques are used to clean and visualize it. Data mining aids in the differentiation of data characteristics based on their properties. Authors in reference [10] investigate a variety of textual features that can be utilized to distinguish between fraudulent and genuine information. They have used these qualities to train a variety of different ML algorithms and ensemble technique, and then evaluate their performance on four real-world datasets. According to reference [11], there are many computer techniques that can be used to identify fraudulent information based on its linguistic content. Authors in references [12,13] have investigated identifying and categorizing bogus news on social media sites like Facebook and Twitter in several studies.

In reference [14], researchers used English media articles from numerous sources, applied clustering method and established fake score for each one to readers. In reference [15], authors exposed multiple views on worldwide news. Their goal is to create a framework that uncovers fake news, encouraging people to make their own decisions about the possibility of fake news. In reference [16], authors largely addressed problems for subjective blogs, and the solution is focused on certain topics or politicians. Extraction of quotations from news items is also carried out. The research reported in reference [17] has a significant impact, thanks to pre-trained word embeddings. They created a ground-breaking strategy for improving the precision of pre-trained word embeddings by combining Word2Vec and GloVe methodologies, lexicon-based approaches, and part-of-speech (POS) tagging techniques. To test and confirm the efficiency of the accuracy improvement, a variety of deep learning models and sentiment datasets were used. In reference [18], authors investigate a unique scalable mechanism for inferring fakes of large number of news sources on social media platforms. Also, they show demographic parameters of news sources.

Depending on the context and study topics under consideration, there are many definitions of false news and its many manifestations. Authors in reference [19] distinguish two high-level categories of false news that deal with news outlets' intentions while publishing articles: ideology and spin. If an outlet fabricates stories to promote a particular point of view on an issue, it is committing ideological fraud. If the media is attempting to generate a memorable narrative, there is likely to be phony spin. A generally used second definition of false news separates three types: coverage, gatekeeping, and assertion. The visibility of topics or entities in media coverage, such as a person or a nation, is referred to as fake coverage. News organizations choose stories to cover through a process known as gatekeeping, often referred to as selection or agenda setting. How writers choose to report on things is the subject of statement fake, also known as presentation fake. For instance, the editorial stance on one presidential candidate can influence the volume and style of a newspaper's coverage of the election, which is a well-known trick during US elections. Authors in reference [19] cover various sorts of fake news in great depth.

6.3 ALGORITHMS

In this section, we explain the algorithms that were employed in this comparative analysis. Naive Bayes (NB), support vector machine (SVM), random forest (RF), decision tree (DT), logistics regression (LR), and passive aggressive algorithm (PAA) are the algorithms used.

6.3.1 Naive Bayes

The NB classifier is selected because it is simple, straightforward to compute, works quickly with huge amounts of training data, and is less sensitive to missing data. Its foundation is a conditional probability model, which, given a problem instance to be classified and a vector $x = (x_{1,...}, x_n)$ reflecting some n qualities, assigns probabilities $p(C_k j, x_{1,...}, x_n)$ to each of K potential outcomes or classes (independent variables). The issue with the above formulation is that if the number of features n is huge or if a feature might have a lot of different values, it is hard to base such a model on probability tables.

The conditional probability can be deconstructed using Bayes' theorem as follows:

$$p(C_k x_j) = \frac{P(C_k) \cdot P(x_j c_k)}{P(x)} \tag{6.1}$$

Assume that for $I = 1, ::: ... \ n - 1$. So, provided the values of the feature variables are known, we may argue that $p(C_k j, x_{1,...}, x_n) = 1/Z \ p(C_k) \ i = 1 - n \ p(x_i j \cdot C_k)$, where the evidence is a scaling factor depending exclusively on a constant.

$$P(E1/E2) = \frac{P(E1) \cdot P\left(\dfrac{E2}{E1}\right)}{P(E2)} \tag{6.2}$$

Here,

$P(E1)$=Probability that event $E1$ will occur.

$P(E2)$=Probability that event $E2$ will occur.

$P(E1/E2)$=The likelihood that event $E1$ will occur given event $E2$.

$P(E2/E1)$=The likelihood that event $E2$ will occur given event $E1$.

6.3.2 Support vector machine

SVM is a powerful method that works in high dimensional space, is very effective, and can handle any data types by changing the kernel. If we want to classify the data points into 'c' classes, the first one-to-rest approach, 'c' SVMs will be used by the classifiers where each SVM would predict the membership in one of the 'c' classes. In the second one-to-rest approach, $c(c - 1)^2$ SVMs will be used by the classifier.

6.3.3 Random forest

Random decision forests handle the issue of decision trees overfitting their training set. According to Tin Kam Ho, who developed the first random decision forest algorithm utilizing the random subspace method, Eugene Kleinberg's stochastic discriminating approach to classification is implemented in this way.

6.3.4 Decision trees

Decision trees are a typical approach for many machine learning applications. Tree learning comes closest to meeting the criteria for being an off-the-shelf technique for data mining since it is invariant under scaling and several other transformations of feature values, is resilient to the insertion of irrelevant features, and offers inspectable models. However, they are rarely precise.

A base node, branches, and leaf nodes make up its tree-like structure. An attribute test is represented by each internal node, a test result is represented by each branch, and a class label is represented by each leaf node. The tallest node in the tree is called the root node. The decision tree approach is a subset of supervised learning. They are applicable to issues requiring regression and classification. The tree representation is used to solve the issue; on the central node of the tree, attributes are recorded, and each leaf node corresponds to a class label. The advantages of this algorithm are as follows:

- The algorithm seldom requires any domain knowledge.
- It is easy to understand.
- The algorithm is simple and fast in terms of the learning and classification process.

6.3.5 Logistic regression

To describe the characteristics of population expansion in ecology, such as how it rises quickly and then approaches the environment's sporting ability, statisticians developed the logistic function, also known as the sigmoid feature. It is an S-shaped regression model that predicts how likely a particular data input will fall into the '1' category. The sigmoid function is used to model the data in LR, much as linear regression assumes that the data follow a linear distribution.

$$g(z) = \frac{1}{1 + e^{-z}} \tag{6.3}$$

6.3.6 Passive aggressive algorithm

PAA, a type of machine learning technique, is commonly used in big data applications. The biggest learning scenarios make the greatest use of them. One of the algorithms for online learning. Unlike batch learning, which uses the whole training dataset all at once, online machine learning algorithms take input data in a sequential manner and update the machine learning model gradually. This is particularly helpful when there is a large quantity of data present, as in our study, and training the full dataset would be computationally impractical due to its size.

6.4 METHODOLOGY

In an effort to identify fake news agencies, we have used text mining and machine learning algorithms. Figure 6.1 depicts the study's overall system design. Seven major western media outlets' news content has been crawled. Once the data has been preprocessed, it is arranged into a form that is helpful.

6.4.1 Data preparation

There is much more to data preparation for ML algorithms than merely cleaning and arranging the data. We gather pertinent data after defining the problem—that is, what precisely is the task at hand, which is fake news detection. As previously noted, we have indexed news stories from seven significant western media sources. Here, both training data and testing data are prepared in the format, which is required by the algorithms. Next exploratory data analysis (EDA) is carried out. This aids in analyzing issues like the kind and distribution of data in each variable, the linkages between variables, and how each variable varies in relation to the result we are hoping to predict or are interested in obtaining. Figure 6.2 shows the data visualization as part of EDA process that is carried out. This is followed by data cleaning and validation. Here, tokenization, stop word removal, and stemming of data are carried out to prepare data for the next steps.

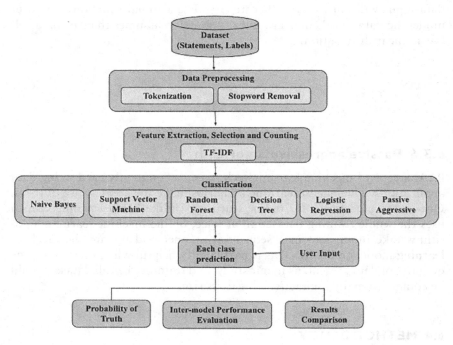

Figure 6.1 Process flow of the proposed methodology.

6.4.1.1 Tokenization

Tokenization is the process of dividing a large block of text into smaller tokens. Here, tokens can take the form of words, characters, or subwords. The three types of tokenization are word, character, and subword (n-gram characters).

6.4.1.2 Stop word removal

Stop word removal is performed after tokenization. Stop words are unimportant words in the language that make a lot of noise. In a sentence, these words are frequently employed. Common words like a, as, about, an, are, at, the, by, for, from, how, in, is, of, on, or, that, the, these, this, too, was, what, when, where, who, will, and others were omitted. These terms were removed from each document before moving on to the next stage of processing.

6.4.1.3 Stemming

We proceed to stemming after removing the stop words. Stemming is the process of stripping a word down to its root, or lemma, which is joined to

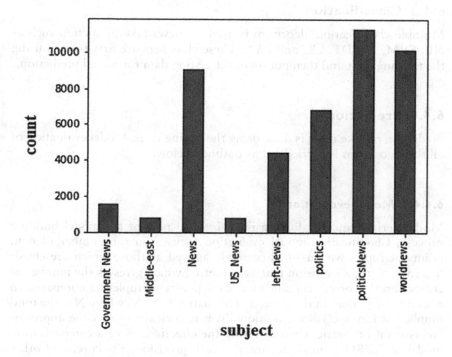

Figure 6.2 Exploratory data analysis.

suffixes, prefixes, or the roots of other words. The data is then sent on to be processed for feature extraction, selection, and counting using the term frequency (TF)–inverse dense frequency (IDF) technique.

6.4.2 TF–IDF

The processed text is vectorized using the TF–IDF. A metric for assessing a word's significance within a corpus is the TF–IDF. A word's frequency in a document is inversely correlated with how important it is, although its frequency in a corpus is directly correlated.

$$TF - IDF = TF * IDF \qquad (6.4)$$

Here,

- *TF*=('w' word occurrences in a document)/(Total words count of document).
- *IDF*=log (Total documents in each corpus/Total documents containing the word 'w').

6.4.3 Classification

Multiple classification algorithm is used for news fake prediction such as NB, SVM, RF, DT, LR, and PAA. These classifiers are first trained using the training data and then put on to the testing data for actual prediction.

6.4.4 Prediction

Prediction of fake news is done using the testing data. Model evaluation of all the algorithms is carried out as outlined below.

6.4.4.1 Model evaluation

Model performance evaluation is an integral part of the model building process. Classification model evaluation focuses on the number of data points or tuples we classified correctly as well as those which are classified incorrectly. Confusion matrix is plotted which gives us the number of correct and incorrect classification data points or tuples as compared to actual target values in the dataset. The matrix is $N*N$, where N is the total number of target classes. Additionally, it is critical to select the appropriate assessment metric when assessing the effectiveness of a categorization model. AUC/ROC curve, accuracy, recall, precision, F1-score, and other well-known metrics are among the accessible ones. Here, we used the following evaluation metrics for the classification models. These are used in the intra-model comparison carried out as shown in Table 6.1.

In the inter-model comparison with the best performing models from this study with existing models, we compare it with Wang [20] and Khanam et al. [2]. Wang used convolution neural network (CNN) and bidirectional long short-term memory networks (Bi-LSTM). Khanam et al. used various ML algorithms such as SVM, KNN, and XGBoost in their study.

Table 6.1 Evaluation metrics used for all models

Accuracy	$\dfrac{TP + TN}{TP + FP + FN + TN}$
F1 Score	$\dfrac{2 \times (\text{Recall} \times \text{Precision})}{(\text{Recall} \times \text{Precision})}$
Precision	$\dfrac{TP}{TP + FP}$
Recall	$\dfrac{TP}{TP + FN}$

6.5 RESULTS

Figures 6.3–6.7 shows the plotted confusion matrix for each model. We carry out counting of most frequent words in real and fake news, and Figure 6.8 depicts the real vs. fake words in the text. We also plot the most frequent words in real and fake news. Figures 6.9 and 6.10 depict the same.

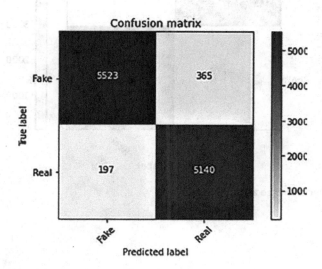

Figure 6.3 Naive Bayes algorithm's result.

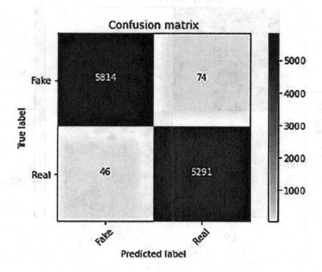

Figure 6.4 Random forest algorithm's result.

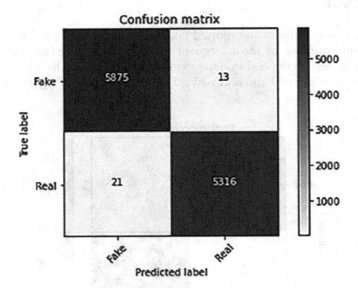

Figure 6.5 Decision tree algorithm's result.

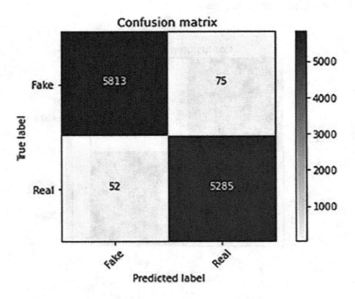

Figure 6.6 Logistic regression's result.

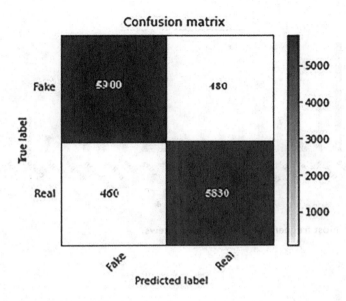

Figure 6.7 PAC classifier's result.

```
target
fake    23481
true    21417
Name: text, dtype: int64
```

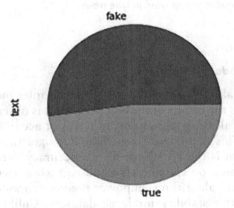

Figure 6.8 Counting most frequent words in real news.

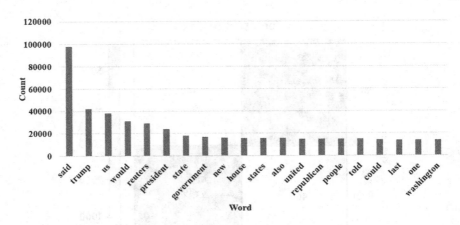

Figure 6.9 Most frequent words used in real news.

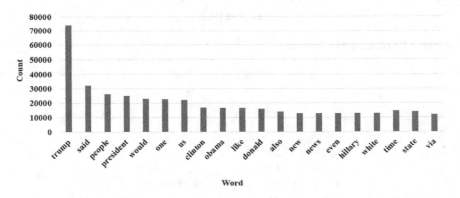

Figure 6.10 Most frequent words used in fake news.

6.5.1 Discussion

6.5.1.1 Intra-model comparison

The accuracy of all the models is carried out in inter-model comparison. Figure 6.11 shows the results of the comparison. It is observed that decision tree outperforms all other algorithms in terms of accuracy by returning a figure of 99%. This is followed closely by RF algorithm. The worst performing algorithm is the PAA with 91.5% accuracy. Since these types of algorithms are based on classification and regression trees (CART), these supervised learning algorithms empower predictive modeling with higher accuracy and better stability for large datasets. Unlike linear modeling techniques, they map nonlinear relationships quite well.

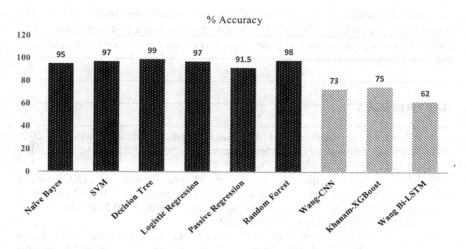

Figure 6.11 Intra-model and inter-model comparision of classifier accuracies.

6.5.1.2 Inter-model comparison

We carry out an inter-model comparison based on the two best performing models from our study with existing models. Wang used CNN and Bi-LSTM. As shown in Figure 6.11, the accuracy achieved is only 73% and 62%, respectively. Khanam et al. used various ML algorithms such as SVM, KNN, and XGBoost in their study. The highest performing model, i.e., XGBoost achieved an accuracy of 75%. In comparison, all the models we used have outperformed these models with decision tree achieving the highest accuracy of 99%.

6.6 CONCLUSION

In this study, we have carried out a benchmark comparison of various ML algorithms to detect fake news from real news. We used six ML algorithms based on different paradigms and benchmark them. From results, it can be concluded that supervised CART algorithms like DT and RF perform good the task of fake new detection from large datasets. In addition, they not only classify a particular type of text, but they can also be generalized for different textual properties to achieve optimum results when exposed to any domain. In the comparison of best performing models developed in this study with existing approaches using CNN, Bi-LSTM and algorithms like XGBoost, it is observed that all the algorithms in the study outperformed these approaches and offered a robust approach to tackle the issue of fake news. As part of future research, the work will be extended to address issues like propagation of fake news, faster fake news computations in real-time/online scenarios via alternative hardware architectures like graphical processing unit (GPU), identifying the source of fake news, etc. toward developing a more robust expert systems for performing real-time fake news identification.

REFERENCES

1. Allcott, H., & Matthew, G. (2017). Social Media and Fake News in the 2016 Election. *Journal of Economic Perspectives*, 31(2), 211–236. https://doi.org/10.1257/jep.31.2.211
2. Khanam, Z., Alwasel, B. N., Sirafi, H., & Rashid, M. (2021). Fake News Detection Using Machine Learning Approaches. *IOP Conference Series: Materials Science and Engineering*, 1099(1), 012040. https://doi.org/10.1088/1757-899x/1099/1/012040
3. Granik, M., & Mesyura, V. (2017). Fake News Detection Using Naive Bayes Classifier. 2017 IEEE First Ukraine Conference on Electrical and Computer Engineering (UKRCON). https://doi.org/10.1109/ukrcon.2017.8100379
4. Buntain, C., & Golbeck, J. (2017). Automatically Identifying Fake News in Popular Twitter Threads. 2017 IEEE International Conference on Smart Cloud (SmartCloud). https://doi.org/10.1109/smartcloud.2017.40
5. Della Vedova, M. L., Tacchini, E., Moret, S., Ballarin, G., DiPierro, M., & de Alfaro, L. (2018, May 1). Automatic Online Fake News Detection Combining Content and Social Signals. https://doi.org/10.23919/FRUCT.2018.8468301
6. Ahmad, I., Yousaf, M., Yousaf, S., & Ahmad, M. O. (2020). Fake News Detection Using Machine Learning Ensemble Methods. *Complexity*, 2020, 1–11. https://doi.org/10.1155/2020/8885861
7. Lazer, D. M. J., Baum, M. A., Benkler, Y., Berinsky, A. J., Greenhill, K. M., Menczer, F., ... Zittrain, J. L. (2018). The Science of Fake News. *Science*, 359(6380), 1094–1096. https://doi.org/10.1126/science.aao2998
8. Chauhan, T., & Palivela, H. (2021). Optimization and Improvement of Fake News Detection Using Deep Learning Approaches for Societal Benefit. *International Journal of Information Management Data Insights*, 1(2), 100051. https://doi.org/10.1016/j.jjimei.2021.100051
9. Nagaraja, A., Soumya, K. N., Sinha, A., Rajendra Kumar, J. V., & Nayak, P. (2021). Fake News Detection Using Machine Learning Methods. International Conference on Data Science, E-Learning and Information Systems 2021. https://doi.org/10.1145/3460620.3460753
10. Ahmad, I., Yousaf, M., Yousaf, S., & Ahmad, M. O. (2020). Fake News Detection Using Machine Learning Ensemble Methods. *Complexity*, 2020, 1–11. https://doi.org/10.1155/2020/8885861
11. Conroy, N. J., Rubin, V. L., & Chen, Y. (2015). Automatic Deception Detection: Methods for Finding Fake News. *Proceedings of the Association for Information Science and Technology*, 52(1), 1–4. https://doi.org/10.1002/pra2.2015.145052010082
12. Vosoughi, S., Roy, D., & Aral, S. (2018). The Spread of True and False News Online. *Science*, 359(6380), 1146–1151. https://doi.org/10.1126/science.aap9559

13. Patankar, A. A., Bose, J., & Khanna, H. (2018). A Bias Aware News Recommendation System. ArXiv:1803.03428 [Cs]. Retrieved from https://arxiv.org/abs/1803.03428

14. Hamborg, F., Donnay, K., & Gipp, B. (2018). Automated Identification of Media Bias in News Articles: An Interdisciplinary Literature Review. *International Journal on Digital Libraries*, 20(4). https://doi.org/10.1007/s00799-018-0261-y

15. Lazaridou, K., Krestel, R., & Naumann, F. (2017, November 1). Identifying Media Bias by Analyzing Reported Speech. https://doi.org/10.1109/ICDM.2017.119

16. Kim, M.-J., Kang, J.-S., & Chung, K. (2020). Word-Embedding-Based Traffic Document Classification Model for Detecting Emerging Risks Using Sentiment Similarity Weight. IEEE Access, 8, 183983–183994. https://doi.org/10.1109/access.2020.3026585

17. Ribeiro, F., Henrique, L., Benevenuto, F., Chakraborty, A., Kulshrestha, J., Babaei, M., & Gummadi, K. (2018). Media Bias Monitor: Quantifying Biases of Social Media News Outlets at Large-Scale. *Proceedings of the International AAAI Conference on Web and Social Media*, 12(1). https://doi.org/10.1609/icwsm.v12i1.15025

18. Mullainathan, S., & Shleifer, A. (2005). The Market for News. *The American Economic Review*, 95(4), 1031–1053. Retrieved from http://www.jstor.org/stable/4132704

19. D'Alessio, D., & Allen, M. (2000). Media Bias in Presidential Elections: A Meta-Analysis. *Journal of Communication*, 50(4), 133–156. https://doi.org/10.1111/j.1460-2466.2000.tb02866.x

20. Wang, W. Y. (2017, July 1). "Liar, Liar Pants on Fire": A New Benchmark Dataset for Fake News Detection. https://doi.org/10.18653/v1/P17-2067

Chapter 7

A comprehensive review of classical and deep learning-based time series models

Ishan G. Gala and Pranav Kulkarni
Marathwada Mitramandal's College of Engineering

CONTENTS

7.1 Introduction   85
7.2 Methodology   86
    7.2.1 Data collection and preprocessing   86
    7.2.2 Time series forecasting methods   87
    7.2.3 Training and performance evaluation   89
7.4 Results   89
7.5 Conclusion   92
References   92

7.1 INTRODUCTION

Time series forecasting is a data science approach that is commonly used in business, supply chain management, inventory planning, finance, and manufacturing. Many prediction problems need time series extrapolation or forecasting as they have a time component. Forecasting time series (Chatfield 2000) is an important topic of machine learning (ML) and may be considered a supervised learning problem. Forecasting is the technique of predicting future observations by fitting models to previous data.

Time series forecasting is the process of forecasting or predicting future values across time (Lim and Zohren 2021). It comprises building models from previous data and then utilizing them to make observations/predictions and guide future strategic decisions based on these results. The future is forecasted or predicted based on what has already been learned using the previous data. The time order dependence between observations is introduced by time series. This reliance is both a limitation and a structure that adds another source of knowledge.

Based on verified historical data, time series models are used to forecast occurrences. Common kinds include ARIMA (Newbold 1983), smooth-based, and moving average (Hansun 2013). Because all models do not provide the same results for the same or similar dataset, it is crucial to determine which model works best based on the unique time series data. Although traditional time series forecasting methods are primarily concerned with

DOI: 10.1201/9781003107767-7

linear correlations, they are complex and perform well in a wide range of situations, providing your data is correctly processed and the algorithm is appropriately designed. Deep learning algorithms (Gamboa et al. 2017) and (Sezer et al. 2020) show great potential for time series forecasting, including learning temporal dependency and handling temporal structures such as seasonality and trends, both of these factors are automated (Gardner and McKenzie 1985). Deep learning architectures (Lara-Benítez et al. 2021) are used in experiments on time series data.

In this manuscript, eight different models, namely, autoregression (AR), autoregressive moving average (ARMA), autoregressive integrated moving average (ARIMA), seasonal autoregressive integrated moving average (SARIMA), simple exponential smoothing (SES), Holt Winter's exponential smoothing (HWES), Prophet, and LSTM (long short-term memory), are trained on stock price data and evaluated using various metrics.

7.2 METHODOLOGY

In this manuscript, different models are used to forecast the price of a stock (Reliance Industries). The time series models are evaluated on performance metrics such as mean absolute percentage error, mean absolute error, mean squared error, and root mean squared error. These metrics are generally used to evaluate the performance of the models. The real-time stock data are used to train and predict future value. The data are fetched using Alphavantage API, which includes the open and close prices of the stock (Idrees et al. 2019) for the past 17 years. We have used close prices for training and testing the models. The stock price data of Reliance Industries Ltd. is chosen to perform a comparison of various time series models. This stock was chosen as Reliance is one of the most reputed and well-recognized companies in the market. Any stock can be chosen to analyze and compare the results, but in this research, Reliance stock price data are used. The models used in the research will directly be tested on the data without any fine-tuning to compare the performance of the models.

7.2.1 Data collection and preprocessing

In this step, the stock data are fetched using the Alphavantage API. The data contain open and close prices of the stock, with various other technical values. To train the model, we create a new data frame that contains the daily close price and the date. This data frame will then be used to train various models and evaluate their performance. It only contains the daily close price of the Reliance stock for the past 17 years. The last day value is excluded while training for comparing the predicted and real value.

7.2.2 Time series forecasting methods

There are mainly two types of methods used in this manuscript for a comprehensive review:

1. Classical time series methods.
2. Deep learning–based methods.

1. **Classical Time Series Methods:**
   a. **Autoregression (AR):**
      An autoregressive model (AR) is used to describe time-varying processes in nature, economics, and other domains, which are a form of the random process. The autoregressive model stipulates that the variable which is used as output is linearly dependent on its own previous values and a stochastic factor, resulting in a stochastic difference equation.

      The AR(p) model is defined as follows:

      $$X_t = \sum_{i=1}^{p} \varphi_i X_{t-i} + \varepsilon_t \tag{7.1}$$

      where $\varphi_1,...,\varphi_p$ are the parameters of the model, c is the constant, and ε_t is the white noise.

   b. **Autoregressive Moving Average (ARMA):**
      Autoregressive moving average models (ARMA) explain a (weakly) stable stochastic process using two polynomials, one for autoregression and one for moving average:

      $$X_t = \varepsilon_t + \sum_{i=1}^{p} \varphi_i X_{t-i} + \sum_{i=1}^{q} \theta_i \varepsilon_{t-i} \tag{7.2}$$

      where $\varphi_1,...,\varphi_p$ are the parameters of the model, c is the constant and ε_t is the white noise, $\theta_1,...,\theta_q$ are the parameters of the model, and μ is the expectation of X_t (often assumed to equal 0).

   c. **Autoregressive Integrated Moving Average (ARIMA):**
      An autoregressive integrated moving average model is a generalization of an ARMA model (Wang and Guo 2020). These two models are used to analyze time series data in order to better understand it and anticipate future points in the series. When data reveal signs of mean nonstationarity, an initial differencing step can be applied one or multiple times to eliminate mean function nonstationarity (i.e., the trend).

   d. **Seasonal Autoregressive Integrated Moving Average (SARIMA):**
      It combines the ARIMA model with seasonal autoregression, differencing, and moving average modeling capabilities.

e. **Simple Exponential Smoothing (SES):**

Exponential smoothing is a very straightforward method for smoothing time series data that makes use of the exponential window function. Compared to the basic moving average which weights previous observations equally, exponential functions utilize weights that decrease exponentially over time. It is a basic process for determining anything depending on the user's previous assumptions, for example, seasonality. Exponential smoothing is often utilized in time series data analysis.

$$s_t = s_{t-1} + \alpha(x_t - s_{t-1}) \tag{7.3}$$

where α is the smoothing factor, and $0 \leq \alpha \leq 1$.

f. **Holt Winter's Exponential Smoothing (HWES):**

The Triple Exponential Smoothing approach, sometimes referred to as Holt Winter's Exponential Smoothing (HWES), models the subsequent time step as an exponentially weighted linear function of the observations from the previous time step while taking seasonality and trends into consideration. Univariate time series with trend and/or seasonal components is suitable for this method. It was used for forecasting stock market prices in New Zealand (Dassanayake et al. 2020).

2. **Deep Learning–Based Methods:**

a. **Prophet:**

Prophet is an open-source time series model building technique that blends old and new ideas. It excels at modeling time series with numerous trends and seasonalities while avoiding some of the limitations of other techniques. It is made up of three time functions plus an error term: growth $g(t)$, seasonality $s(t)$, holidays $h(t)$, and error e_t:

$$y(t) = g(t) + s(t) + h(t) + \epsilon_t \tag{7.4}$$

The growth function replicates the general trend of the data. The previous notion should be known to anybody with a rudimentary grasp of logistic and linear functions. The novel notion in Prophet is that the growth trend might be present at all data points or changed at "changepoints."

The seasonality function s(t) is just a time-dependent Fourier series. Think of the Fourier series as the sum of many successive sines and cosines if you are unfamiliar with it. Each sine and cosine phrase is given a coefficient. This total, in the instance of Prophet, may mimic almost any curve or seasonality in our data.

The holiday capability allows Prophet to update predicting when a holiday or large event changes the predicted results. When every day is incorporated in the forecast, it takes a list of dates and adds/subtracts value from the estimate depending on past data on the recognized holiday dates. You may also define a range of days based on dates (for example, the time between Christmas and New Year's, holiday weekends, and Thanksgiving's relationship with Black Friday/Cyber Monday). It has already been used to forecast stock prices and compared to other ARIMA models (Garlapati et al. 2021).

b. **LSTM (Long Short-Term Memory):**

The recurrent neural network (RNN)-based LSTM (long short-term memory) architecture is frequently utilized in natural language processing and time series forecasting. The LSTM solves a significant short memory problem that affects RNNs. Based on a probabilistic model, LSTM employs a succession of 'gates', each with its own RNN, to keep, forget, or ignore data items. LSTM (Mehtab et al. 2020) is compared to ARIMA, and the results demonstrate that LSTM outperforms ARIMA (Siami-Namini et al. 2018).

LSTMs may also be used to solve exploding and vanishing gradient issues. These problems develop as a result of the periodic weight modifications made by a neural network as it learns. Gradients become larger or smaller when there is epochs repetition, and with each change, the gradients of the network become simpler to compound in either direction. As a result of this compounding, the gradients are either far too big or far too little. While standard RNNs have severe limitations such as exploding and disappearing gradients, the LSTM design considerably mitigates these concerns.

7.2.3 Training and performance evaluation

The above models are trained on the data frame that we created in Section 7.2.1 now, the models have to predict a value that will be compared with the actual value for evaluations.

7.4 RESULTS

For the evaluation of the machine learning algorithms on the stock price prediction analysis, the following metrics were considered:

1. **MAPE**—MAPE stands for absolute percentage error, also known as mean absolute percentage deviation sometimes, it is a measure of prediction accuracy of a forecasting method in statistics.

2. **MAE**—MAE stands for 'mean absolute error', a common metric used for the evaluation of machine learning algorithms, and the closer it is to zero, the better the algorithm is at predicting unknown quantities.
3. **MSE**—MSE stands for mean squared error. It is the average of the square of the difference between the original values and the predicted values.
4. **RMSE**—RMSE stands for root mean squared error. It is the standard deviation of the prediction errors. They indicate how far the data points are located from the regression line.

Table 7.1 shows the comparison of different metrics for each model. LSTM appears to be the best among the others.

Table 7.1 Comparison table

Sr.No.	Models	MAPE	MAE	MSE	RMSE
1.	AR	4.178	105.682	11168.790	105.682
2.	ARMA	5.219	132.036	17433.525	132.036
3.	ARIMA	5.328	134.783	18166.569	134.783
4.	SARIMA	5.328	134.783	18166.569	134.783
5.	SES	5.322	134.631	18125.506	134.631
6.	HWES	5.321	134.631	18125.506	134.630
7.	Prophet	8.249	208.702	43556.509	208.702
8.	LSTM	2.199	43.562	3050.603	55.232

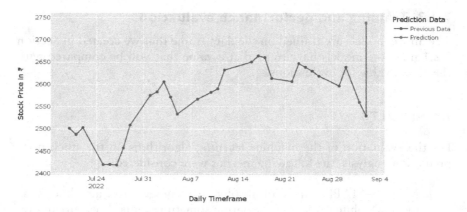

Figure 7.1 Stock price prediction using Prophet.

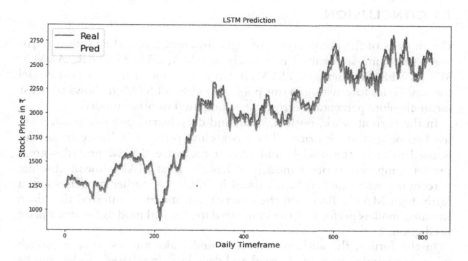

Figure 7.2 **Stock price prediction using LSTM.**

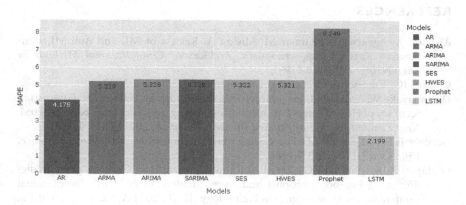

Figure 7.3 **Mean absolute percentage error of models.**

Figure 7.1 shows the prediction results given by the Prophet. The prediction is shown in red whereas the actual values are shown in blue.

Figure 7.2 shows the prediction results given by LSTM. The prediction results are compared with actual data.

Figure 7.3 shows the mean absolute percentage error of different models. LSTM has the lowest MAPE.

7.5 CONCLUSION

On analysis of the performance of eight different classical and deep learning–based time series models, namely ARIMA, SARIMA, AR, ARMA, SES, HWES, Prophet, and LSTM, it can be concluded that the best model for time series forecasting in this pool of models is LSTM. It shows the least mean absolute percentage error when compared to other models.

In the current work, both classical and deep learning–based models are used to predict stock prices. The stock close price of Reliance Industries is used to train the models and predict the price. LSTM provides great results compared to other models. It has the least MAPE (mean absolute percentage error) of 2.19%, as listed in Table 7.1. Other models show a fairly high MAPE. Based on the observation, it can be inferred that deep learning models perform better compared to classical models for stock price prediction.

In the future, the authors intend to undertake an ensemble approach wherein a combination of classical and deep learning–based models can be used to develop a model to predict stock prices. AutoML solutions (Alsharef et al. 2022) can be tested and performance comparison can be done with classical models and find out the difference in their working.

REFERENCES

Alsharef A, Aggarwal K, Kumar M, Mishra A. Review of ML and AutoML solutions to forecast time-series data. *Archives of Computational Methods in Engineering*. 2022 Jun 1:1–5.

Chatfield C. Time-series forecasting. Chapman and Hall/CRC; 2000.

Dassanayake W, Ardekani I, Jayawardena C, Sharifzadeh H, Gamage N. Forecasting accuracy of Holt-Winters Exponential Smoothing: Evidence from New Zealand. *New Zealand Journal of Applied Business Research*. 2020;17(1): 11–30.

Gardner Jr ES, McKenzie ED. Forecasting trends in time series. *Management Science*. 1985 Oct;31(10): 1237–1246.

Garlapati A, Krishna DR, Garlapati K, Rahul U, Narayanan G. Stock price prediction using Facebook prophet and Arima models. In 2021 6th International Conference for Convergence in Technology (I2CT) 2021 Apr 2 (pp. 1–7). IEEE.

Hansun S. A new approach of moving average method in time series analysis. In 2013 Conference on New Media Studies (CoNMedia) 2013 Nov 27 (pp. 1–4). IEEE.

Idrees SM, Alam MA, Agarwal P. A prediction approach for stock market volatility based on time series data. *IEEE Access*. 2019 Jan 25;7:17287–17298.

Lara-Benítez P, Carranza-García M, Riquelme JC. An experimental review on deep learning architectures for time series forecasting. *International Journal of Neural Systems*. 2021 Mar 16;31(03): 2130001.

Lim B, Zohren S. Time-series forecasting with deep learning: A survey. *Philosophical Transactions of the Royal Society A*. 2021 Apr 5;379(2194): 20200209.

Mehtab S, Sen J, Dasgupta S. Robust analysis of stock price time series using CNN and LSTM-based deep learning models. In2020 4th International Conference on Electronics, Communication and Aerospace Technology (ICECA) 2020 Nov 5 (pp. 1481–1486). IEEE.

Newbold P. ARIMA model building and the time series analysis approach to forecasting. *Journal of Forecasting*. 1983 Jan;2(1):23–35.

Sezer OB, Gudelek MU, Ozbayoglu AM. Financial time series forecasting with deep learning: A systematic literature review: 2005–2019. *Applied Soft Computing*. 2020 May 1;90: 106181.

Siami -Namini S, Tavakoli N, Namin AS. A comparison of ARIMA and LSTM in forecasting time series. In 2018 17th IEEE International Conference on Machine Learning and Applications (ICMLA) 2018 Dec 17 (pp. 1394–1401). IEEE.

Wang Y, Guo Y. Forecasting method of stock market volatility in time series data based on mixed model of ARIMA and XGBoost. *China Communications*. 2020 Apr 7;17(3): 205–221.

Chapter 8

Use of technologies in media and communication

Interventions of artificial intelligence in mitigating fake news on social media

Santosh Kumar Biswal, Ambika Sankar Mishra, and Narsingh Majhi
Rama Devi Women's University

CONTENTS

8.1 Introduction   95
    8.1.1 Social media effects: A paradox   97
8.2 Existence of false news on digital social media outlets   98
8.3 The effects of fake news on news values in journalism   101
8.4 Artificial intelligence in curbing fake news on social media   102
    8.4.1 Natural language processing strategies   102
    8.4.2 Deep-learning AI algorithms   103
    8.4.3 Locating and identifying fraudulent bot accounts   105
    8.4.4 Digitalizing the process of curbing fake news: A mixed bag 105
8.5 Concluding remarks   107
References   109

8.1 INTRODUCTION

Conspiracy theories and fake news are all part of daily life in contemporary times. These days, it is quite difficult to tell the difference between true and incorrect information. Since much information is consumed electronically, false information can frequently have a substantial negative impact on someone's health or financial situation. In blogs, emails, social networks, or online media, anyone can contribute content. However, because of the sources' disparate areas of expertise and points of view, the material is getting heterogeneous. On a variety of subjects, information that is inconsistent and contradictory is getting published by the politicians, opinion leaders, and occasionally scientists. Cybercriminals use the Internet as an efficient and affordable means of disseminating information that benefits their goals (Ahmed et al., 2021). Anyone can post anything online and there is no quality control. Most of the time, the accuracy of material found on online platforms has not been verified.

DOI: 10.1201/9781003107767-8

Fake news has always existed throughout the entire history of humanity (Burkhardt, 2017). However, the vast majority of people have accepted the truth because they have either directly observed the facts—such as when items fall—or because the facts have been publicized by trustworthy individuals. Of fact, even today, persons with a good reputation might spread misleading information owing to sheer ignorance. The majority of people were unable to immediately determine whether the earth was spherical or flat, but they accepted the information as true since it was provided by individuals, they trusted due to their credentials, positions, etc. The overwhelming majority of people respected the authority of scientists, religious leaders, and political figures. The majority came to this conclusion using the recognized methods, such as printed books, teacher-led sessions, and scholarly lectures. These processes served as the consensus's instruments and protocols.

Social media usage has unquestionably increased rapidly over the years. As researchers try to better understand the effects of using social networking sites (SNSs), this growth has received a significant deal of academic interests (Verduyn et al., 2017). Today's online world has a serious problem with fake news. Through online social media sites, false information is easily spreading at a faster pace. Therefore, it is crucial to stop the dissemination of false information.

Social media platforms, which include a number of well-known ones like Facebook, YouTube, Twitter, and Instagram have grown to be popular interactional tools in the field of digital communication. Together, these numerous platforms have significantly increased the user access and interaction, as well as communication and interaction among users. The usage of personal technical gadgets with ever-increasing user convenience for social media interaction is on the rise (Vriens & van Ingen, 2018). At the same time, the amount of content available has multiplied, giving the customers a huge selection of media content from which to select based on individual preferences (Milla & Mataruna-Dos-Santos, 2019).

The uses and gratification of people who use the social media outlets are getting enhanced and unique as well. Audiences are getting more aware of the medium of communication. As a result, they are choosing the medium for maximizing their level of gratification. Understanding and reassessing the importance of such medium of communication is a kind of revisiting the uses and gratification theory. People today display themselves on a variety of platforms, allowing the users to change their presence and appearance while interacting with others about their interests, values, and points of view. Social engagement and connectivity were the main goals of social media platforms in the beginning, but now that social life is being mediated by these personal acts, there is an increase in individualized behavior on these new social spaces (Feldman & Hakim, 2020). The connected research raises the issue of how fake news affects society. Fake news can influence and mislead entire populations, governments, or even just a small portion of the population.

8.1.1 Social media effects: A paradox

Social media effects remain a paradox. Despite the fact that social media has immensely expanded, positive benefits have not been equally realized in the society. Social media uses and their advantages are distributed unequally in society, resulting in unequal access of distribution. SNSs are being debated in the context of elderly and the uneducated than others (Kozerska, 2015). Indeed, researches have revealed that how people utilize the Internet and its many platforms reflects structural differences in societal institutions. Due to access limitations, digital inequality has come to the fore and is getting ceaselessly debated.

Social media has permeated every aspect of public life because its use and relevance in daily life have skyrocketed. The use of social media is not limited to social contact, rather it is used for job advancement, civic engagement, and leveraging consumption objectives. In this regard, social media's diversification of multiple use cases reveals how much these online public spaces have politicized, commercialized, and individualized. However, these online social spaces are far from being inclusive of all people in this regard (Watkins, 2011). Various players are pursuing a wide range of economic and societal gains from their use, including common users from different socio-demographic groups within a given community, corporations, organizations, political movements, and the platforms themselves. These many social media features have become significant parts of people's life, albeit they are not equally prevalent throughout the spectrum of demographic groups.

There are some pronounced age inequalities, which follow a trend comparable with earlier Center studies on social media usage. According to 84% of persons aging from 18 to 29, and 81% of adults aging from 30 to 49, social media is something they regularly use. Although the disparities between younger and older Americans vary between the platforms, these age differences typically extend to the use of particular platforms, with younger Americans being more likely than their older counterparts to utilize these sites (Pew Research Centre, 2021). One study reveals that social media uses indicating substantial overlap between what is done and what is to be done in Finland. Additionally, research demonstrates how the users of these platforms are affected by the commodification and politicization of online social spaces. Despite having a same set of social media use objectives, disparities in activity levels, popularity, and connections to physical environments were discovered among populations (Koiranen et al., 2020).

8.2 EXISTENCE OF FALSE NEWS ON DIGITAL SOCIAL MEDIA OUTLETS

Fake news is existing on the social media platforms. As fake news spreads like wildfire on social media outlets, it is difficult to track and controls them. The three concepts of misinformation, disinformation, and mal-information are frequently combined in fake news (Santos-D'Amorim & Miranda, 2021). Some of the fake news is based on political, ideological, or commercial motivations, while others are just for the purpose of fun. However, they do it with a purpose. Some people spread false information with the knowledge that it is false and with a purpose. Different people have different motives. Some of disseminators feel proud to share the fake news. While some do it for fun, others believe that they must inform people of the significance of the news.

Numerous events have had an effect on society, contributing not only benefits but also dangers in various cases. The fake news remains today's most contentious issues due to the threat it poses to society. The authors' findings in the article illustrated the false news phenomenon's contemporary significance, which is recognized as a significant global trend with relevance to many scientific areas (Alonso García et al., 2020). The Internet is just the most recent medium of communication to be misused to disseminate lies and false information; propaganda has been for ages. The oxygen, heat, and fuel that a fire requires to burn are symbolized by the fire triangle. Similar to this, bogus news needs three essential components to be successful. These together make up the fake news triangle; without any one of them, it cannot propagate and fail to reach its intended audience. The abundance of online information makes the issue worse. The cost and access of consuming and creating various information materials have flooded the information industry (Menczer & Hills, 2020).

The situation is made worse by the fact that search engines and social networking websites offer customized recommendations based on the large amounts of information about users' historical preferences to which they have access. They give higher priority to content in our feeds that we are most likely to agree with, regardless of how extreme, and they keep us away from content that might cause us to reconsider our thoughts. We are therefore simple prey for polarization.

Social media sites like Facebook, Twitter, YouTube, and Instagram not only display content that aligns with our views but also popular content at the top of our screens and statistics on how many people have liked and shared a particular item. Few of us are aware that these indicators do not offer impartial evaluations of quality. In fact, political echo chambers on Twitter are so strong that it is not possible to anticipate a user's political views with a high degree of accuracy; we share the same views as most of your contacts. This chambered design effectively disseminates information within a community while shielding it from outside organizations.

According to Shu et al. (2017), fake news intentionally leads the consumers to embrace erroneous beliefs that are disseminated to advance particular agendas, which have negative effects on people and society. For organizations and corporations, the spread of fake news presents serious issues. In reality, false information can be purposefully spread to deceive consumers by endorsing a particular viewpoint or opinion about a service, organization, or brand.

Recent studies have also observed that how fake news affects organizations and brands (Cheng & Chen, 2020; Visentin et al., 2019). Such incorrect information may hurt retailers' interests by dissuading customers from making purchases. On the other hand, people may be duped into purchasing particular products based on false reviews, which are recognized as a kind of Internet forgeries (Martens & Maalej, 2019). So, in the age of social media, issues of fake news are galloping because of the factors like user-generated content and contents without attributions. The nature of fake news is that it spreads fastly. Obviously, it is hard to detect and curb misinformation. Misinformation has long-term effects. People tend to purposefully or unintentionally build their arguments based on their exposure to the nature of information.

The primary reason is that erroneous information persists, though, is that people are prone to confirmation bias, naive realism, and truth bias. People who are inherently 'truth-biased' have "the presumption of truth" when interacting with others and "the tendency to judge an interpersonal message as truthful, and this assumption is probably amended only if anything in the scenario generates scepticism," according to research (Rubin, 2017). Social media users frequently have no idea that there are postings, tweets, articles, or other written materials whose only objective is to mold others' opinions in order to influence their judgments. Precisely, information manipulation occurs because of poor knowledge of the subjects on the part of social media users. Again, some of the young users are indulged in breaking news.

Disinformation has always been a part of combat and military planning. However, it is certainly becoming worse as a result of social media and smart technology use. This is because modern communication technologies offer a generally inexpensive, low-barrier means of disseminating information. Technology firms and social media businesses are focusing on network analysis, machine learning, and natural language processing to detect bogus news automatically. In order to reduce the likelihood that consumers would encounter "fake news," an algorithm is supposed to recognize information as such and rank it lowers.

Bombardment of same information again and again increases the likelihood that someone will believe it from a psychological standpoint. The circle of reinforced information consumption behaviors can be broken when AI recognizes falsehood and decreases the frequency of its dissemination. However, AI detection is still not trustworthy. First, the trustworthiness of the detection is determined by evaluating the language (content) and its social network. The basic issue is that how AI authenticates the true nature of the content, despite being able to identify the origins of fake news and their distribution pattern.

AI-backed grouping algorithm should theoretically be able to determine if information comprises any form of false information or not if there is enough training data. Doing such differences, however, actually requires prior political, cultural, and social knowledge or common sense, which natural language processing algorithms presently is lacking of. A preprint investigation demonstrates that fake information can also be exceedingly complex when the information purposefully changed to "look as real news yet including misleading or manipulative content."

The theme has a significant impact on classification analysis since AI frequently distinguishes subjects based on them rather than on the issue's actual content. For instance, articles about COVID-19 are more likely than articles about other topics to be classified as fake news. Employing and motivating human resource to work with AI to confirm the accuracy of evidence is one solution. In other cases, limiting the dissemination of fake news might be seen as censorship and a danger to the right to free speech. The right to free speech has been considered at the same time. Even a human could struggle to distinguish between bogus and real information. Therefore, perhaps the most important question is: Who or what defines fake news? How can we be confident that AI filters will not lead us into the false positive trap and mistakenly identify material as phony due to its linked data?

In the application of fake news, AI system might be sinister. For an instance, authoritarian governments may utilize AI as a defense to remove any items or to pursue criminal charges against anyone who disagrees with the ruling class. Therefore, any use of AI—as well as any pertinent laws or metrics which are the outcomes of its pragmatic uses—will call for unbiased system with an outside observer. Future obstacles still exist since disinformation is a persistent problem, particularly when it is connected to foreign intervention. Future fake news may not be detectable by an algorithm created today. Deep fakes, for instance, which are "extremely realistic and difficult-to-detect digital modification of audio or video," are probably going to be more prevalent in information warfare in the future. Additionally, end-to-end encryption used by messaging apps like WhatsApp and Signal makes it more challenging to monitor and intercept the transmission of false information.

To regulate this, a balance must be struck between personal protection, privacy, and the suppression of misinformation. The use of AI to combat misinformation is unquestionably worthwhile, but given the potential consequences, caution and openness are required. Regrettably, new technical solutions might not be a panacea. In a view to combat the disinformation, funding needs to be initiated for the universities, research institutes and other think tanks and knowledge bodies.

8.3 THE EFFECTS OF FAKE NEWS ON NEWS VALUES IN JOURNALISM

Any media organization or online network that knowingly disseminates misleading material is in violation of the ethics of journalism. Furthermore, spreading lies through conventional, social, and online media with such malevolent motives is a crime against humanity that breeds disorder, conflict, crises, illness, corruption, and squalor. It completely ignores the importance of news and violates accepted standards of journalism. We are already extremely familiar with the selection criteria for information as information producers and consumers, and we know why some topics are interesting while others are not. We can also observe how journalists choose their sources and how it affects how the general audience interprets the news.

The concept of news values was initially put forth in 1965 by Galtung and Holmboe Ruge. Since then, it has gone through numerous adjustments in reaction to the Internet revolution and the advent of new journalistic genres. However, the assumption of truthful information underpins all concepts of news values. News' primary characteristic is that it builds its story on actual happenings. Meanwhile, the emergence of fake news has been a problem for us lately. The quantity of disinformation portals, fake news publishers, and social media posts have increased on the Internet.

Fake news is produced in a way that gives the impression that it is reliable information. Outside of the media and communication industries, this trend is harmful. Even more worrisome are its prospective impacts on schooling at all levels. Online sources are often viewed by students as important, current, and generally trustworthy sources of knowledge and data. There are fewer trustworthy network sources for e-learning and education as a result of diverting attention away from the reliability of news sources, which also diminishes the reliability of information sources on the Internet as a whole. Although incorrect, inaccurate, or twisted information has always existed, the Internet has greatly increased its devastating potential (Gurba et al., 2019). Understanding their creation and dissemination becomes increasingly crucial for scholars, media users, and educators.

8.4 ARTIFICIAL INTELLIGENCE IN CURBING FAKE NEWS ON SOCIAL MEDIA

Fake news is usually disseminated through yellow journalism. However, the advent of the Internet has multiplied the extent of fake news. The most important step in stopping the viral of fake news and saving people's lives is early fake news identification. Unknowingly, people spread false information and participate in it. While those who first propagate false information do so with the intention of harming innocent individuals. Fake news detection and its pattern of dissemination are becoming extremely important to society and the government in order to stop this string of events. It is important to analyze the motivations behind Internet posts and develop the ability to identify what is true from what is fake.

8.4.1 Natural language processing strategies

The users can compute quantitative metrics and employ natural language processing strategies to help us identify false news by adhering to the ideas of human cognition and behavioral sciences. For instance, the limited capacity model of mediated motivated message processing postulates that our brain must use distinct cognitive strategies to process different structural and functional aspects of a text. In other words, not all texts are created equal.

Artificial intelligence can be positioned to play a significant role in halting the spread of disinformation. One of the new technologies that has altered how people view business concerns is artificial intelligence (Palanivelu et al., 2021). Businesses outlet are increasingly using machine learning and sophisticated analytics to solve difficulties. Natural language processing (NLP) is evolving in the age of artificial intelligence, opening up a wealth of options for organizations interested in deciphering human sentiments from the data already available (Kang et al., 2020). All forms of social and natural communication can be used with NLP. Text mining has been helping to identify numerous, relevant trends in the textual collection. By strategically utilizing NLP in today's market environments, organizations can gain an edge over rivals. The vast amounts of unstructured data in a variety of fields can be fought with the aid of artificial intelligence and natural language processing. Natural language processing makes it possible for people and machines to communicate more effectively, which improves strategy and decision-making and overall corporate efficiency (Bahja, 2020).

Natural language describes how people communicate, including speech, text, and emotions. People are more engaged when speaking than when writing (texting) (Eisenstein, 2019). The capacity of people to withstand, assess, and make complex judgments based on the amount of data created by humans and robots nowadays is vastly outnumbered. Analyzing human behavior is one of the biggest difficulties that organizations face. A simple method for integrating chatbots to advance business growth is provided by business intelligence (Vashisht & Dharia, 2020).

A predictive false news model has also been created using machine learning techniques. The writers take a methodical approach to identify false news by examining the many characteristics of it. Number of programs or technologies that are used to distribute fake news. They involve the most widely used programs, including Facebook, Twitter, and WhatsApp. These are the primary channels via which fake news spreaders might reach unsuspecting people (Igwebuike & Chimuanya, 2020). Moreover, technologies based on computational linguistic technique is used to analyze the language used by the US Twitter users who spread lies (Li & Su, 2020).

ConvNet-RNN hybrid technique and the LSTM model were utilized to differentiate between fake news and true news in order to detect fake news (Ma & Tan, 2021). Users can choose to use NLP and a random forest algorithm to distinguish between reliable news and unreliable news. Based on relational features directly extracted from the text, such as sentiment, entities, and facts, a semantic false news detection method is used. It is found that including semantic qualities significantly enhances accuracy in using brief texts with varied degrees of truth (Braşoveanu & Andonie, 2021).

8.4.2 Deep-learning AI algorithms

In the Chrome environment, an autonomous false news detection algorithm is shown that can identify bogus news on Facebook. Additionally, the authors use a number of Facebook account-related factors and a few news item aspects to evaluate the activity of the account using deep learning (Sahoo & Gupta, 2021). Here, bogus news is identified by using machine learning algorithms. When it comes to fake news, AI has been a paradox. While intelligent robots help to spread this type of information automatically, machine learning algorithms help to automatically detect it (Ruediger et al., 2017; Meneses Silva et al., 2021). A branch of artificial intelligence known as machine learning employs algorithms that can identify patterns from data sets in order to anticipate future data or make decisions. Numerical variables derived from pertinent characteristics define the learning data (Murphy, 2012).

By enabling the identification of the "core story" in the content and locating other variations in the consolidated pool of content, artificial intelligence offers substantial value. Cross-posts and later iterations of the same narrative would be easy for AI agents to find, as well as references, user discussion threads, and complaints—from multiple sources, in different languages, and with varying degrees of quality.

When enough people vote and factcheck a story, AI generalizes the results to all known variations of the story and various types of coverage, enabling quantification of the reliability of both the core story and its variants. AI components identify the patterns and continuously check each story for new occurrences and facts that require verification. All of these are preserved in the immutable content store along with tagged content, evaluations, publisher ratings, and metadata that are eternally archived as a part of world history. No "phantom" fake news or deletions have ever occurred.

The new technology is automatic: The new AI system, according to researchers, "is totally automated and can readily recognise 90% of bogus news." He claimed that many news outlets frequently utilize the same news for different purposes. Choosing which news information is accurate when it is published and transmitted simultaneously is challenging. The new instrument can serve as a standard in such a circumstance.

The ability of artificial intelligence is to produce information that is startlingly human-like improves every year. Language models like GPT-3 are capable of producing complete articles on their own with just a one-line prompt as input. Deepfakes—false images or videos—are frequently produced using deep neural networks. Video editing used to be a time-consuming, expensive procedure that required advanced technical knowledge. The technology is now more widely available because to open-source programs like FaceSwap and DeepFaceLab (Masood et al., 2022). Today, utilizing a computer or a mobile device, anyone with a basic level of knowledge may quickly make deep fakes. For billions of people, the Internet has emerged as the primary source of information. Our opinions and perspectives are shaped by what we read and see online. Information access is essential for democracy. Fake news repeatedly tampers with the truth and is killing democracy one cut at a time.

Deep neural networks, made up of two complementary components, are known as generative adversarial networks. A generator algorithm attempts to mimic the patterns in a set of real samples—text or images—as input to produce synthetic examples. Contrarily, the discriminator algorithm develops the ability to distinguish between authentic and artificial samples. Both the discriminator and the generator constantly advance as they seek to outsmart one another. The final step creates a generator that can create synthetic samples that cannot be distinguished from actual ones.

The recently released GPT-3 by OpenAI can produce technical manuals, business notes, emails, poems, and other types of writing. It can translate between languages, clarify legal papers, and provide philosophical answers. It is nearly impossible to distinguish between human-written text and GPT-3 output for short texts. The validity of the information mentioned in an article, independent of whether a human or a computer produced it, can be used as a second way to spot fake news. Human editors are used by services such as Snopes, Politifact, and FactCheck, to conduct research and speak with primary sources to confirm a claim or an image. Additionally, these services are relying more and more on AI to assist them in shifting through vast amounts of data.

8.4.3 Locating and identifying
fraudulent bot accounts

When it comes to finding and removing problematic, illegal, and undesired Internet content, AI technologies have shown to be extremely helpful in information operations. AI-based bot-spotting and bot-labeling techniques have been effective in locating and identifying fraudulent bot accounts. By identifying accounts that have been known as bots, social media businesses are assisting the users in better understanding the content they are engaging with and assessing its legitimacy for themselves. More effort must be done, though, for detection algorithms to be as accurate as email spam filter technologies.

Almost all the social media outlets have started using algorithms to get free from trolls. Facebook asserts that bogus news is recognized by AI technologies. Pattern recognition, which is closely related to machine learning and AI, allows us to recognize risky online behavior. By studying previously flagged articles that users and fact checkers classified as unreliable, AI can be used to find the patterns of terms that can identify phony stories. For the time being, fully automatic fact checking is still far off. The most common duties on social media networks are still handled by AI, while the more difficult ones are still reviewed by humans.

False information can be located and eliminated using AI technologies. In reality, by recognizing the patterns using a variety of algorithms over the past few years, AI has successfully been able to differentiate between human and machine-generated content. Another aspect of some AI-powered analytical tools that can be used to determine whether or not a headline and article body are compatible is the capacity to categorize stances. This is performed by reading the material carefully and analyzing the writing style.

Since fake news travels rapidly on social media outlets, Facebook, Google, Twitter, and YouTube have teamed up to combat it and propagate official rules on their platforms. Even before COVID-19, start-ups like MetaFact were using AI to track and identify bogus news in real time. The objective of the fact-checking websites is to assist the journalists in their fight against false information, not to take over their work. MetaFact aims to provide a trust layer for the Internet by utilizing AI (Sachdev, 2020). As the first of a series, the start-up is introducing AI into newsrooms to help the journalists validate news and provide enriched reporting by lowering the cost, time, and effort necessary to do so with a lower risk of error. AI tools will aid the journalists in their fight against the expanding issue of fake news by providing direct access to privacy, data interoperability, and cognitive computing skills.

8.4.4 Digitalizing the process of curbing
fake news: A mixed bag

The spread of false information online is nothing new. However, it has spread more widely as a result of the quick development of ICTs, particularly the use of AI tools. In order to verify the accuracy of the content, fact check-ing has historically relied significantly on manual human interaction. As disinformation is increasing very fast, it is difficult to handle manually to this sheer extent. In this context, AI tools enjoy the advantages of being automated, cost effective and fast paced. However, AI too suffers from shortcomings.

AI tools are both an efficient means of producing fake news content and a potent weapon against it. Deep fakes in particular look incredibly lifelike and are challenging for even experts to spot. The accuracy of any informa-tion source can soon be verified by users thanks to AI-based automated technologies like machine learning, deep learning, and natural language processing. Needless to say, AI tools have wider applications in mitigating the fake news. Although AI-powered technologies have numerous benefits, they can push the human rights and democratic political processes at the stake. It is now well acknowledged that AI applications have two sides. There are a number of drawbacks when automated systems are used to curb misinformation. The potential over-blocking of accurate and lawful content is the first significant problem with AI's "over inclusion" func-tion. Despite the fact that technology is continually developing and evolv-ing, AI models are nevertheless susceptible to false negatives and positives, which means that occasionally they may wrongly classify legitimate data and accounts as fake. False positives can have a serious impact on the right to free speech and expression which ultimately affect the society in a bad manner.

The automated systems' ability to assess the truthfulness of particular claims is still somewhat constrained. Only basic declarative assertions, lacking inferred claims, or claims hidden within complex sentences that are easy for humans to understand are currently recognized by AI systems. The same is true for terms that require details about a particular culture or area. Because they have not yet understood core human concepts like sar-casm and irony, AI systems are unable to handle more sophisticated forms of deception. Language barriers and regional disparities in the political and cultural context make this problem more challenging.

Additionally, certain AI tools automate the human prejudices that are unfavorable for members of a particular group. No matter how objective we would want our technology to be, observers have noted that in the end, its effectiveness is determined by the people who develop it and the data it is fed. Poor, insufficient, or unrepresentative training data, as well as the pri-orities and values of the programmers who design and train the algorithms, can all contribute to algorithm bias.

AI-based solutions raise important questions about who should be in charge of deciding whether content is appropriate or inappropriate, legal or illegal, and desirable or undesirable. Should legal authorities, Internet platforms, or public bodies—whether or not institutionally connected to governments—determine the legitimacy of and demand the immediate deletion of online content? While advancements in AI technologies will undoubtedly aid to the users who protect against harmful material operations on digital platforms, they present an opportunity for adversaries to temporarily expand the breadth and effectiveness of their operations.

8.5 CONCLUDING REMARKS

In a view to combat the disinformation, human resource and funding need to be initiated for the universities, researcher institutes and other think tanks and knowledge bodies. In combating the upcoming disinformation onslaught, society must be resilient. The government, citizens, and other stakeholders of the society are to be concerned about the proliferation of fake news online. Fake news is being created for the purpose of distrust which have the bearings on social and cultural dynamics (Wardle & Derakhshan, 2017).

The key to battle with fake news on social media is the comprehending objectives for both the users and the platform itself. One can frequently see advertisements that are customized to one's interests or search history because social media platforms generate money by selling user data to ad businesses. On social media, fake news could be impossible to ignore. However, by exercising critical thinking, one can prevent the spread. Keep an appropriate amount of curiosity about the content you see on social media, be aware of how platforms curate what you see, and frequently engage in research. When used properly and thoughtfully, social media can be a tremendous tool for both individuals and businesses.

Even while there are numerous strategies for preventing fake news on social media, they occasionally fall short. Since there are no editors on social media, any content can be shared without being checked. The users of social media must also play a significant part. By mastering the research process for determining the truth behind the phony information, we may become the editors instead of requiring the social media corporations to take the necessary action. The first and most important step in defending our society against this fraudulent content is taking responsibility for oneself.

The flood of information in our social networks is making it nearly hard to distinguish between credible and false sources. It can be challenging to distinguish between legitimate news and fraudulent news on social media. In order to trick us into believing fake news is authentic, malicious actors take advantage of our psychology. Emotions can, however, have an impact on our psychology as well. Social networks are seen as sources of "large-scale emotional contagion" since studies have shown that content with a high emotional level is more contagious. Our psychology becomes less reasonable when we are exposed to information with a strong emotional component, which reduces our capacity to distinguish between what is true and what is untrue.

In order to identify false news, the users can compute quantitative measures and use natural language processing techniques by adhering to the theories of human cognition and behavioral sciences. The signs of false information can be regularly tracked. We can evaluate the extent to which the various types of false information deviate from accurate news in terms of the cognitive effort needed to analyze the content. Be wary of content that lacks proper grammar and vocabulary.

The spreaders of false information are aware that when you surf social media, you will not put as much effort into it as you would in other circumstances; after all, you came there to learn something or have fun, not to work. Support the need for caution when using social networks, specifically, and for the ability to recognize when someone is attempting to exploit our psychology against us. Both individual and collective work must be done for this. Public decision-makers need to pay closer attention to the population's disturbingly low levels of media literacy. Technology is developing much more quickly than our psychology, educational systems, or political decision-making. If we do not make a greater effort to address the issues we currently face as well as those that lie ahead, this will cause issues for our societies.

False information evokes emotions considerably more strongly than accurate news. In fact, their sentiment is ten times more negative. Additionally, this is crucial as they appeal 37% more to the reader's morality (World Economic Forum, 2022). There are numerous strategies to spot bogus news and maintain proper information. It frequently displays a blatant prejudice and may attempt to elicit strong emotions from the readers. Verification is the most crucial method in this case because such content could originate from unreliable news sources. Both conventional methods of verification and online tools must be used to check the bogus news.

The conventional method of verification expressly entails consulting the primary source and having it verified. It can be sourced via emailing the individual or organization, reviewing various original papers related to the story, or both. The information must then be verified by at least one more source, and this technique must also be used for online verification. For online verification procedures, there are specific tools and approaches. Again, we can use the image to perform a reverse image search on Google or any other search engine to confirm an image or a photo and determine whether it is real or fraudulent. If the photograph has already been used, it can tell. It also reveals the image's age and whether or not it has been utilized in other settings. Additionally, if a fact-checker has previously reported on the subject, that piece will also display. A video of bogus news is also verified using the same procedure.

Augmented reality, virtual reality, blockchain, metaverse, and other immersive technologies are coming in a big way which will influence the practice of journalism. Society needs to be cautious while using these technologies in social media platforms. Technologies cannot be blindly used for economic interests. Of course, the political economy of technologies plays a vital role and these aspects must be factored in to critically assess the usefulness of technologies in general and AI in social media outlets in particular. In this context, the political economy of artificial intelligence can be visited.

To conclude, technology and human nature are both equally to be blamed for the issue of fake news. We must alter human behavior to fit our new responsibilities as big-information consumers in order to tackle this problem. Credibility and sincerity are crucial, and we must learn to value them. This is a gradual awakening that we hope will happen someday; it will not happen overnight. Until then, technology can mitigate the effects and spur this shift.

REFERENCES

Ahmed, A. A. A., Aljabouh, A., Donepudi, P. K., & Choi, M. S. (2021). Detecting fake news using machine learning: A systematic literature review. *arXiv preprint arXiv:2102.04458*.

Alonso García, S., Gómez García, G., Sanz Prieto, M., Moreno Guerrero, A. J., & Rodríguez Jiménez, C. (2020). The impact of term fake news on the scientific community. Scientific performance and mapping in Web of Science. *Social Sciences*, *9*(5), 73.

Bahja, M. (2020). Natural language processing applications in business. *E-Business-Higher Education and Intelligence Applications*. DOI: 10.5772/intechopen.92203

Braşoveanu, A. M., & Andonie, R. (2021). Integrating machine learning techniques in semantic fake news detection. *Neural Processing Letters*, *53*(5), 3055–3072.

Burkhardt, J. M. (2017). History of fake news. *Library Technology Reports*, *53*(8), 5–9.

Cheng, Y., & Chen, Z. F. (2020). The influence of presumed fake news influence: Examining public support for corporate corrective response, media literacy interventions, and governmental regulation. *Mass Communication and Society*, *23*(5), 705–729.

Eisenstein, J. (2019). *Introduction to natural language processing*. MIT Press.

Feldman, Z., & Hakim, J. (2020). From Paris is burning to# dragrace: Social media and the celebrification of drag culture. *Celebrity Studies*, *11*(4), 386–401.

Gurba, K., Kaczmarczyk, D., & Pajchert, B. (2019). Fake news as a threat for news values in communication and education. In *INTED2019 Proceedings* (pp. 6937–6945). IATED.

Igwebuike, E. E., & Chimuanya, L. (2020). Legitimating falsehood in social media: A discourse analysis of political fake news. *Discourse & Communication*, *15*(1), 42–58.

Kang, Y., Zhang, F., Gao, S., Lin, H., & Liu, Y. (2020). A review of urban physical environment sensing using street view imagery in public health studies. *Annals of GIS, 26*(3), 261–275.

Koiranen, I., Keipi, T., Koivula, A., & Räsänen, P. (2020). Changing patterns of social media use? A population-level study of Finland. *Universal Access in the Information Society, 19*(3), 603–617.

Kozerska, A. (2015). Life satisfaction among people aged 60 and over, participating in restricted social networks in Poland: Related variables. *Problems of Education in the 21st Century, 67*, 29.

Li, J., & Su, M. H. (2020). Real talk about fake news: Identity language and disconnected networks of the US public's "fake news" discourse on Twitter. *Social Media+ Society, 6*(2), 2056305120916841.

Ma, F., & Tan, G. (2021). NLP in fake news detection. In *IRC-SET 2020* (pp. 71–83). Springer.

Martens, D., & Maalej, W. (2019). Towards understanding and detecting fake reviews in app stores. *Empirical Software Engineering, 24*(6), 3316–3355.

Masood, M., Nawaz, M., Malik, K. M., Javed, A., Irtaza, A., & Malik, H. (2022). Deepfakes generation and detection: State-of-the-art, open challenges, countermeasures, and way forward. *Applied Intelligence, 53*, 1–53.

Menczer, I., & Hills, T. (2020, January). Information Overload Helps Fake News Spread, and Social Media Knows It. Retrieved from https://www.scientificamerican.com/article/information-overload-helps-fake-news-spread- and-social-media-knows-it/

Meneses Silva, C. V., Silva Fontes, R., & Colaço Júnior, M. (2021). Intelligent fake news detection: A systematic mapping. *Journal of Applied Security Research, 16*(2), 168–189.

Milla, A. C., & Mataruna-Dos-Santos, L. J. (2019). Social media preferences, interrelations between the social media characteristics and culture: A view of Arab nations. *Asian Social Science, 15*(6), 71–77.

Murphy, K. P. (2012). *Machine learning: A probabilistic perspective.* MIT Press.

Palanivelu, P., Sukumaran, R., Kumar, S. H., & Jogarao, D. V. S. (2021, June). A Review of Technical Literature and Trends Related to Automotive Engine Modelling by ANN. In *2021 International Conference on Design Innovations for 3Cs Compute Communicate Control (ICDI3C)* (pp. 71–77). IEEE.

Pew Research Centre. (2021, April 7). Social Media Use in 2021. Retrieved from https://www.pewresearch.org/internet/2021/04/07/social-media-use-in-2021/

Rubin, V. L. (2017). Deception detection and rumor debunking for social media. In *The SAGE Handbook of Social Media Research Methods.* SAGE. https://uk.sagepub.com/en-gb/eur/the-sage-handbook-of-social-media-research-methods/book245370

Ruediger, M. A., Grassi, A., Freitas, A., Contarato, A. D. S., Taboada, C., Carvalho, D., ... & Traumann, T. (2017). Robôs, redes sociais e política no Brasil: estudo sobre interferências ilegítimas no debate público na web, riscos à democracia e processo eleitoral de 2018.

Sachdev, R. (2020, April). Towards Security and Privacy for Edge AI in IoT/IoE Based Digital Marketing Environments. In *2020 Fifth International Conference on Fog and Mobile Edge Computing (FMEC)* (pp. 341–346). IEEE.

Sahoo, S. R., & Gupta, B. B. (2021). Multiple features based approach for automatic fake news detection on social networks using deep learning. *Applied Soft Computing*, *100*, 106983.

Santos-D'Amorim, K., & Miranda, M. K. F. O. (2021). Misinformation, disinformation, and malinformation: Clarifying the definitions and examples in disinfodemic times. *Encontros Bibli: revista eletrônica de biblioteconomia e ciência da informação*, *26*, 1–23.

Shu, K., Sliva, A., Wang, S., Tang, J., & Liu, H. (2017). Fake news detection on social media: A data mining perspective. *ACM SIGKDD Explorations Newsletter*, *19*(1), 22–36.

Vashisht, V., & Dharia, P. (2020). Integrating chatbot application with qlik sense business intelligence (BI) tool using natural language processing (NLP). In *Micro-Electronics and Telecommunication Engineering* (pp. 683–692). Springer.

Verduyn, P., Ybarra, O., Résibois, M., Jonides, J., & Kross, E. (2017). Do social network sites enhance or undermine subjective well-being? A critical review. *Social Issues and Policy Review*, *11*(1), 274–302.

Visentin, M., Pizzi, G., & Pichierri, M. (2019). Fake news, real problems for brands: The impact of content truthfulness and source credibility on consumers' behavioral intentions toward the advertised brands. *Journal of Interactive Marketing*, *45*(1), 99–112.

Vriens, E., & van Ingen, E. (2018). Does the rise of the Internet bring erosion of strong ties? Analyses of social media use and changes in core discussion networks. *New Media & Society*, *20*(7), 2432–2449.

Wardle, C., & Derakhshan, H. (2017). Information disorder: Toward an interdisciplinary framework for research and policymaking. The Council of Europe, Strasbourg Cedex.

Watkins, S. C. (2011). Digital divide: Navigating the digital edge. *International Journal of Learning and Media*, *3*(2), 1–12.

World Economic Forum (2022). Disinformation is a growing crisis. Governments, business and individuals can help stem the tide. Retrieved from https://www.weforum.org/agenda/2022/10/how-to-address-disinformation/

Chapter 9

Robust color image watermarking using IWT and ensemble model with PCA-based statistical feature reduction

Sushma Jaiswal and Manoj Kumar Pandey

Guru Ghasidas Central University

CONTENTS

9.1 Introduction   113
9.2 Basic terminology   117
   9.2.1 Integer wavelet transform or lifting wavelet transform
       (IWT/LWT)   117
   9.2.2 Random subspace-KNN (RS-KNN)   117
   9.2.3 Bagging method   117
   9.2.4 Principal component analysis (PCA)   117
9.3 Proposed color image watermarking scheme   118
   9.3.1 Watermark embedding process   118
   9.3.2 Watermark extraction process   120
9.4 Result and discussion   122
   9.4.1 Selection of threshold value   123
   9.4.2 Imperceptibility test   123
   9.4.3 Robustness test   124
   9.4.4 Comparative study   127
9.5 Conclusion   130
References   130

9.1 INTRODUCTION

With the addition of digital data on the internet daily, securing digital content through some methods is imperative. Digital image watermarking is one of the methods to secure digital content over the network. Securities of digital content are one of the prime concerns for everyone, and therefore the concept of watermarking is of utmost importance. In image watermarking, the cover image is altered in such a way that the identity of an image can be

DOI: 10.1201/9781003107767-9

proven when it is needed. Image cryptography is also a means of providing security to the color image. However, it is lacking in the sense that once the image is decrypted, and it can be copied without any hassle. Steganography also provides security to the color image, but it requires much computational power, even for adding tiny information [1].

Image watermarking can be of two types based on visibility, i.e., visible and invisible. In the proposed scheme, invisible watermark is implemented. In the proposed scheme, only a color watermarked image is needed for the watermark extraction; therefore, it is a blind watermarking scheme. A watermarking scheme could be fragile, semi-fragile, and robust depending on its robustness. While a semi-fragile watermarking system can tolerate some degree of image distortion, a fragile watermarking scheme cannot. The most amount of picture attacks can be tolerated with robust image watermarking. In the last few decades, image watermarking has emerged as an optimal solution for digital security. Image quality, robustness, capacity, and security are essential requirements of an image watermarking system. The principle of image watermarking says that the quality of the watermarked image must remain good to reveal that the image has been watermarked. Imperceptibility is a measure used to ensure the quality of the watermarked image; robustness is used to check the robustness against most image attacks. Imperceptibility is measured using peak signal-to-noise ratio (PSNR), whereas robustness is calculated using normalized coefficients (NC) and bit error rate (BER). One of the challenges for any watermarking system is to keep a good balance between imperceptibility (PSNR) and robustness (NC and BER) [2].

Different watermarking schemes have been proposed in literature [3] using machine learning and deep learning techniques along with image transformations like the discrete wavelet transform (DWT), discrete cosine transform (DCT), discrete Fourier transform (DFT), fast Fourier transform (FFT), and integer wavelet transform (IWT), among others. Each of the transformation methods has its advantages and disadvantages. Spatial domain–based watermarking is less effective than frequency domain–based image watermarking as it can tolerate more image distortion [3]. Whenever an image is watermarked using a frequency domain–based method, a cover image is first transformed into some frequency to get the matrix of the coefficients. Then, embedding is done based on performing some quantization on the obtained matrix of coefficients. IWT-based watermarking is getting very popular among researchers because of its ability to tolerate more image attacks than any other conventional method. In IWT, an image is represented in terms of the integer value and takes less energy; therefore, it is more efficient [3]. Machine learning-based image watermarking performs better against various image attacks than non-ML-based methods. ML-based methods can learn the patterns based on some relationship between the pixel of watermarked images, and these relationships remain intact even after attacks [4]. Most of the image watermarking reported in the literature extracts the watermark bits based on binary classification techniques. Watermarking can also be done based on image segmentation [5]. In the literature, various ML-based watermarkings are reported by Fu and Shen [6], Verma et al. [7], Islam et al. [8], Chang et al. [9], Sharma et al. [10], Anand et al. [11], Sinhal et al. [12], Jaiswal and Pandey [13] and Barlaskar et al. [14].

Verma et al. [7] developed a lifting wavelet transform (LWT or IWT) and support vector machine-based grayscale image watermarking, in which 12 statistical features have been taken into consideration for feature reduction using PCA. Using twelve feature sets, the binary watermark is extracted using SVM with RBF kernel. The size of the cover image is 512*512, and the size of the binary watermark is 32*16. Twelve feature sets, including skewness, entropy, kurtosis, mean, median, mode, covariance, standard deviation, etc., are calculated from the image coefficient of size 2*2 and $T=11$ gives the optimal results in terms of balancing imperceptibility and robustness. SVM is used for the classification of binary data. It works better when a jpeg attack with a high compression ratio is used, but it still has to be improved in rotation and translation.

Another IWT and SVM-based grayscale image watermarking has been proposed by Islam et al. [8] for analyzing the performance of the different 64 subbands. Out of 64 subbands, 9 subbands have been selected to cover all the subbands. The signature (original) and reference watermark of each 512 bits are used for SVM training and testing. Seven subbands give the optimal performance in terms of imperceptibility and robustness. Twelve statistical features were taken into consideration for training the SVM, and feature selection rather than feature reduction was used. The average imperceptibility achieved is 44 dB for all the subbands.

A DCT-2DLDA-based blind watermarking scheme for the color image has been proposed by Chang et al. [9]. In this scheme, a color image is converted into YIQ color space during the watermark embedding process, and the image is transformed using DCT transform. Here, two binary watermarks, namely, the reference watermark and logo image watermark, are added to the particular bits of the coefficient. Keys are used at various levels to strengthen the system's security, and various features are obtained from the image to train the model. The result shows that the scheme is robust against most image attacks, and it shows imperceptibility of 44.49, 44.78 and 44.38 dB for standard images Lena, baboon, and peppers in case of no attack.

Sharma et al. [10] have proposed an IWT-SVD-based color image watermarking scheme, in which a cover image of size 512*512 and 1024*1204 is decomposed up to the fourth level, and then singular value decomposition (SVD) is applied for watermarking color images. Three types of datasets, i.e., general, medical, and aerial, have been used for watermarking. Artificial bee colony (ABC) optimization has been used to select the best threshold value for watermarking embedding to balance the imperceptibility and robustness.

Anand et al. [11] have proposed the DWT-SVD-based nonblind gray-scale medical image watermarking to add extra security watermark image is encrypted and compressed before watermark embedding. For study purpose cover image of size 512*512, an image watermark of size 256*256 and a text watermark of size 12 characters is considered. Chaotic_LZW and Hyperchaotic-LZW encryption and compression technique is used for image watermarking. The highest PSNR value 44.1944 dB is noticed for the Hyperchaotic-LZW technique.

Blind grayscale image watermarking using IWT and random-subspace one-dimensional linear discriminate analysis has been proposed by Jaiswal and Pandey [13] (RS-1DLDA). Twelve statistical features are taken into account in the proposed work to create a feature set from 512 blocks of size 2*2. Testing and training are done using the signature and reference watermark. Here, the watermark is extracted by binary classification using the RS-1DLDA. In the absence of attacks, it attains an imperceptibility of 35.47 dB for the Lena image, 35.14 dB for the Mandril image, and 35.51 dB for the peppers image.

Ensemble-based watermarking, described by Bingham [15], combines the advantages of multiple machine learning models to provide results that are more robust than those of other ML models. A good watermark extraction can be achieved using the benefit of ensemble machine learning, specifically the random subspace-KNN method. This study uses the Bagging ensemble model and the random subspace-KNN model with and without feature reduction to demonstrate blind nonvisible color image watermarking. The proposed work's goal is to evaluate how well the suggested system defends against various image attacks. The contribution of the proposed work is as follows:

- The suggested work is blind, thus neither a cover image nor a watermark are necessary.
- The security of the system is increased by the use of keys at several levels.
- The watermarked image is more resistant to various image attacks when IWT is used for image decomposition.
- For watermark extraction, using an ensemble-based ML technique yields good results in terms of imperceptibility and robustness.
- Performance of ensemble-based ML models for feature reduction and without feature reduction is proposed.
- The proposed system is compared against similar existing methods and found robust against most image attacks.

The structure of this paper is as follows: Introduction is covered in Section 9.1, the fundamental ideas of the study are covered in Section 9.2, the proposed watermarking method is covered in Section 9.3, the experimental findings and discussion are included in Section 9.4, and the conclusion and future application are covered in Section 9.5.

9.2 BASIC TERMINOLOGY

This section deals with the basic terminology used in the proposed paper.

9.2.1 Integer wavelet transform or lifting wavelet transform (IWT/LWT)

In order to save time and memory for image decomposition, the Sweldens proposed IWT or LWT in 1966 [16]. In contrast to other decompositions like DFT, FFT, and DWT, IWT decomposition treats the coefficient as an integer rather than a float. IWT is made up of three steps, namely, Split, Predict, and Update, and has the benefit of saving energy while dissecting an image. IWT is a good option for image watermarking because of its energy compaction feature.

9.2.2 Random subspace-KNN (RS-KNN)

Random subspace-KNN is an ensemble method based on K nearest neighbor and bagging technique. In the RS-KNN method, a subspace is selected randomly using features space, and then classification is done based on the combining results from multiple classifiers. A new set of k nearest neighbors are computed when a random subspace is selected, RS-KNN based image watermarking has been proposed by Zhang et al. [17] in the year 2019, in which binary watermark extraction is done based on the RS-KNN method. More details on RS-KNN can be found in Ho [18].

9.2.3 Bagging method

The bagging classification method is an ensemble method in which the decision tree learner is used, and the bag ensemble method is used for the classification. In this method, 30 learners are used for classification purposes. A random sample of data is generated from the training datasets, and results are combined once the training is done. It is one of the most commonly used ensemble methods.

9.2.4 Principal component analysis (PCA)

One of the most used methods of feature reduction is PCA. The basis of PCA is the idea that elements that are irrelevant or unnecessary should be excluded. PCA is also known as singular value decomposition (SVD) and empirical orthogonal function (EOF) method [19]. PCA is very popular among researchers, and it can drastically improve the results by selecting the most optimal features.

9.3 PROPOSED COLOR IMAGE WATERMARKING SCHEME

The embedding and extraction techniques are demonstrated in this portion of the paper. The binary classification method is used in this instance to tackle watermark extraction. For the binary classifications, the RS-KNN ensemble machine learning technique is utilized together with bagging. A cover picture is transformed using IWT to the third level for the purpose of embedding a watermark. The resultant 64*64 coefficients are then shuffled using keys from K1 and decomposed into a 1024 matrix of size 2*2. Utilizing seed key K2, the obtained matrixes are again shuffled. Signature watermark image of size 16*32 (512 bits) and randomly generated watermark bits are concatenated and reshuffled using secret seed key K3. For every 1024 matrix, the two most significant coefficients are calculated and the quantization is applied to embed the shuffled watermark bits into the original cover image. For watermark extraction, again decompose the cover image into the third-level IWT transform as done in the embedding process and then calculate the fourteen features like Skewness (ft1), Kurtosis (ft2), Block-Entropy (ft3), Block-Standard deviation (ft4), Block-Mean (ft5), Block- Variance (ft6), Block-Mode (ft7), Block-Median (ft8), Block-Covariance (ft9), Block-Poisson probability distribution (ft10), Block-Moment (ft11), and Block-Quartiles (ft12), Coff_diff_1 (f13), and Coff_diff_2 (f14). A feature set of size 512X14 is created by adding up the values of all the LH3 blocks that correspond to the embedded reference watermark. These feature sets are then provided to the PCA in order to minimize the feature set. The result of the PCA is the feature set, and the training feature set is reduced by the PCA to 512*6 features, where *rd* is the total number of reduced features. The feature vector is increased in size by the matching block coefficient until it is (512*10), at which point one target variable (bit 0 or 1) is added as BAGGING, making RS-KNN supervised in nature. RS-KNN method has been selected for watermark extraction because the selection of a random subspace ensemble boosts the accuracy of the trained KNN model. The outcomes of numerous decision trees trained on various subsets of the columns in the training dataset can be combined using the random subspace model. Here feature set is taken as used by Verma et al. [7] and the feature set is derived from Chang et al. [9]. The testing pattern is generated similarly using the bits where the signature information is embedded.

9.3.1 Watermark embedding process

A watermark (w_{mR}) of length l_{wr} in the proposed technique is divided into two parts i.e. the reference component (Ref_r) of length l_{ref} and the signature component (Sig_r) of length l_{sig}. Using the confidential seed key K3, the reference watermark is created and scrambled at random. A single watermark consisting of the signature and reference components has been combined and is denoted by the symbol W of length N_w as shown in equation 9.1.

$$W = \text{Ref}_r + \text{Sig}_r = w1 + w2+,\ldots,+w_l\text{ref} + w_l\text{ref} + 1+,\ldots,+w_l\text{ref} + l_{\text{sig}}. \quad (9.1)$$

Here, the training set is created using the reference watermark, and the testing pattern set is created using the signature (original) watermark.

The watermark bit 1 and bit 0 can be added using the following formula: If watermark bit is equal to 1, then

$$\cof(n)_i = \cof(n)_i + TH, if\, \text{Diff}^{\max} < \max(\sigma, TH),$$

$$\text{Else}\, \cof(n)_i = \cof(n)_i \quad\quad (9.2)$$

And, if the watermark bit=0

$$\cof(n)_i = \cof(n)_i - \text{Diff}^{\max} \quad\quad (9.3)$$

Here, TH displays a threshold, and $\text{Diff}^{\max}$ displays the difference between the two biggest values of the corresponding i^{th} block. The following is a representation of the average difference in coefficient value σ for all N_{all} blocks:

$$\sigma = \frac{\sum_{i=1}^{Nw} \text{Diff}_i^{\max}}{N_{all}} \quad\quad (9.4)$$

Here, N_{all} in this case refers to all LH3 subband blocks containing watermark bits.

Figure 9.1 shows the color image embedding procedure and the steps for the embedding process are listed as follows:

Step 1. Read the cover image and extract the blue component of cover image.

Step 2. Get the blue component third-level LH3 subband in the size 64*64 using IWT. Step 3. Utilizing the secret seed key K1, arrange the LH3 subband coefficients.

Step 4. Utilizing the non-overlapping coefficients of the LH3 subbands, create a block of size 2*2.

Step 5. To shuffle the acquired 1024 blocks, use the secret seed key K2.

Step 6. using equation 9.4 obtain the average coefficient difference σ.

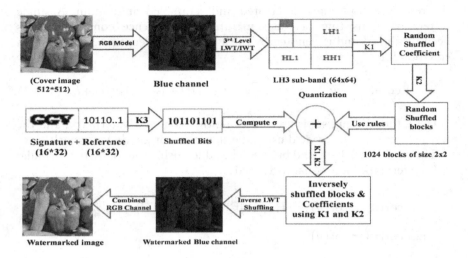

Figure 9.1 Color watermark embedding procedure.

Step 7. Create a 1-D array of the binary watermark (W) of length N_{all} by concatenating the reference watermark (randomly produced) and signature (original) watermarks. Then use seed key K3 to shuffle the bits.

Step 8. Do the following for all N_{all} bits of binary watermark.

7a. Determine each blocks two largest coefficients say $cof(n)$ and $cof(n-1)$.

7b. If the watermark bit is 1, then use equation 9.2 to change $cof(n)$

7c. If the watermark bit is 0, then use equation 9.3 change $cof(n)$

Step 9. Inversely shuffle all the updated blocks and coefficients using the same seed key used in steps 2 and 4 and then perform the inverse IWT transform. Then combine the Red, Green and Blue component together to get color watermark image.

9.3.2 Watermark extraction process

The proposed watermarking system treats the extraction of the watermark as a binary classification problem, classifying a binary bit (0 or 1) using two ensemble-based methods, namely, BAGGING and RS-KNN algorithm. It is very clear from the review of the literature that the ensemble-based machine learning method has an excellent capacity to classify binary bits. The associations between pixels have been seen to be untouched by attacks on images; as a result, this can be used to make logical classifications. The watermark extraction training set of size 512*11 and the testing set of size 512*10 is extracted from the watermarked image. The training

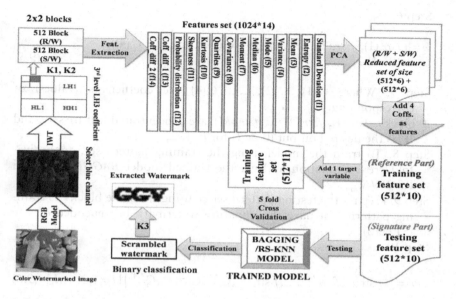

Figure 9.2 Color image watermark extraction procedure.

set is constructed using the reference watermark bits, and similarly, the testing set is constructed using the signature (original) bits. Here *decision tree* learner with *30* learners is used for *the bagging* method, and RS-KNN, the number of *subspace* chosen is *5*, *the number of the learner is 30*, and the learner type is *nearest neighbors*. The learning rate is *0.1* for both ensemble methods.

The process for removing watermarks from colored images is depicted in Figure 9.2, and the procedures are as follows:

Step 1. Retrieve the blue component of 512*512 watermarked images and get the third stage LH3 subband of blue component.

Step 2. Keeping the same secret seed key K1 and blocks with the same seed key K2, reshuffle the integer coefficient of the LH3 subbands.

Step 3. Create feature set $(\{fst_i(k)|k=1, 2, \dots RD\})$ of blocks that includes the reference detail.

Step 4. Apply PCA to get the concentrated feature set $(\{Fstr_i(k)|k=1, 2, \dots M\})$

where $M \leq RD$

Step 5. The training feature set φ has size (512*11) when the coefficients and embedding bits (desired output W_i) of the corresponding blocks are added.

Step 6.

$$\omega = \{((fstr_i(1),\ fstr_i(2),\ ...,\ fstr_i(M),\ C_i(1),\ C_i(2),\ ....,\ C_i(4)),$$
$$W_i | i = 1,\ 2,\ ...,\ l_r\} \tag{9.5}$$

Step 7. Where $C_i(1)$, $C_i(2)$, ..., $C_i(4)$ are coefficients (values) of corresponding.

i^{th} blocks, $fstr_i(1)$, $fstr_i(2)$, ... $fstr_i(M)$, are concentrated feature sets, and W_i is the desired output (0 or 1) for $i = 1, 2, ..., l_r$.

Step 8. To train the model using the training pattern set, apply five-fold cross validation and get the trained model $BAGGING_{train}$ and $RS\text{-}KNN_{train}$.

Step 9. Prepare the testing pattern set φ' using the same blocks as training pattern that have the signature watermark bits encoded of size (512*10).

Step 10.

$$\omega' = \left\{ \left(f\, str_i'^{(1)},\, f\, str_i'^{(2)}, ..., f\, str_i'^{(M)}, C_i'^{(1)}, C_i'^{(2)}, ..., C_i'^{(4)} \right) \Big| i = 1,2,...,l_s \right\} \tag{9.6}$$

Step 11. Extract the 1-D array w' using trained model $BAGGING_{train}$ and $RSKNN_{train}$ and testing pattern set φ'.

Step 12. Reshuffle the bits of 1-D array w' using seed key K3 and reshape w' into the original logo watermark size.

9.4 RESULT AND DISCUSSION

The outcome of the suggested algorithm is covered in this section of the paper, along with its robustness and imperceptibility under various attack scenarios. For the experiment, eight standard color images, including Lena, Peppers, and Mandril of size 512*512, 24 bit/pixel, and a binary watermark image of size 32*16 are used. The majority of the standard images were gathered from [20]. The i5 Intel processor and Matlab 2016a running on the Windows 7 operating system are used to implement the suggested algorithm. Using NC, BER, and PSNR, the stability of the suggested method is examined. The PSNR, which is calculated using mean square error, is used to determine how similar the original cover image and the watermark image are to one another (MSE). PSNR is calculated as shown in equation 9.7. MSE is calculated as shown in equation 9.8, NC is calculated as shown in equation 9.9, and BER is calculated as shown in equation 9.10:

$$PSNR = 10 \log_{10} \frac{255^2}{MSE} \tag{9.7}$$

$$MSE = \frac{1}{M * N} \sum_{ij=0}^{MN} CI(i,1) - WI(i,j) \tag{9.8}$$

$$NC = \frac{\sum_i CI_{ij} \sum_j WI_{ij}}{h \, X \, w} \tag{9.9}$$

$$\text{Bit Error Rate} = \frac{W \, r \, B}{hi * wi} \tag{9.10}$$

Here, CI is cover image, WI is watermarked image, and CI_{ij} and WI_{ij} are value at (i, j), and they are stored as 1 if the watermark bit is equal to 1 and –1; otherwise, hi and wi are the respective dimensions of the watermark image. WrB is incorrectly detected bits. The color test images utilized for the study are displayed in Figure 9.3.

9.4.1 Selection of threshold value

As discussed in the earlier section of the paper, keeping a balance between imperceptibility (PSNR) and robustness (NC and BER) is one of the challenges of image watermarking. In this regard, the selection of optimal threshold value (TH) must be optimal to keep a good balance between these two. Using a larger threshold value decreases the PSNR of watermarked images but increases the robustness and vice-versa; therefore, it is of utmost importance to analyze and select the best threshold value from a given range of threshold values. The optimal threshold value $TH = 32$ has been selected for the experiment purpose.

9.4.2 Imperceptibility test

This section of the paper shows the imperceptibility of the watermarked image using the proposed watermarking scheme. Eight standard images, including Lena and peppers, are used for the experiment. Watermarked images and corresponding imperceptibility value (PSNR) are shown using

Figure 9.3 Color test images: (a) Lena, (b) Peppers, (c) Mandril, (d) Jetplane, (e) House, (f) Lake, (g) Car, and (h) Zelda.

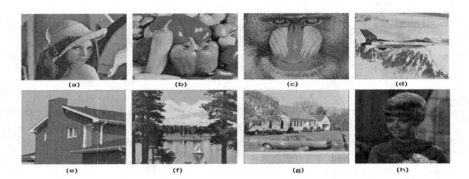

Figure 9.4 Watermarked color test images: (a) Lena, with PSNR=37.83dB, (b) Peppers, with PSNR=37.20dB, (c) Mandril, with PSNR=36.43, (d) Jetplane, with PSNR=37.26dB, (e) House, with PSNR=34.72dB, (f) Lake, with PSNR=36.58dB, (g) Car, with PSNR=36.98dB, and (h) Zelda with PSNR=36.56dB.

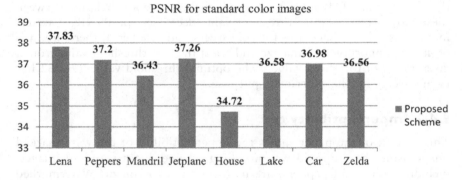

Figure 9.5 PSNR value of different standard images used for experiment.

Figure 9.4. Figure 9.5 shows the PSNR value of different standard images used for the experiment.

9.4.3 Robustness test

Robustness is one of the essential measures for any watermarking image system, and it is measured in terms of NC and BER. In the proposed work, watermark extractions are performed for mentioned eight standard images. NC value against various image attacks for proposed ensemble models, i.e., Bagging and RS-KNN, has been shown using the table below. The proposed ensemble model is tested for various image attacks like Salt and pepper (SLP), Gaussian (GS), Speckle (SPLN), Cropping (CROP), Scaling (SCL), JPEG compression (JPEG), and Rotation (RT) attacks.

Tables 9.1–9.4 show the performance of the proposed ensemble models for eight standard images against various image attacks with PCA (with feature reduction) and without PCA (without feature reduction). In the table, the bold value shows the good performance among the model in case of with PCA and without PCA. The bold and italic value shows the superior performance for particular image attacks. The tables show that the performances of the proposed ensemble models are good enough to resist various image attacks and using PCA may improve the result in some case; however for some image attacks the performance of without using PCA is also good. The proposed model performs well against most image attacks, especially SLP, SPLN, and SCL image attacks. However, it is not performing well against JPEG, CROP and RT image attacks. This could be because JPEG, CROP, and RT image attacks affect the pixels in such a way that it affects the training dataset, so extraction is compromised. The best NC value for SLP (0.01) attack for the bagging model is 0.9648 for Jetplane image without reducing the features, and for the RS-KNN model is 0.9688 for the Lena standard image without reducing the features; likewise, the best NC value for SLP (0.02) attack for the bagging model is 0.9140 for Lake without reducing the features, and for RS-KNN model 0.8867 for Lena without reducing the features. The best NC value for GS (0.01) attack for bagging model is 0.8594 for Lake and for RS-KNN model 0.8359 for Lake without reducing the features. Likewise, the best NC value for the SPLN (0.01) attack for bagging

Table 9.1 NC value of extracted watermark for Lena and Mandril with PCA and without PCA

| Image attacks | Lena | | | | Mandril | | | |
| | With PCA | | Without PCA | | With PCA | | Without PCA | |
	Bagging	RS-KNN	Bagging	RS-KNN	Bagging	RS-KNN	Bagging	RS-KNN
SLP (0.01)	**0.9150**	0.7696	0.9023	*0.9688*	0.9218	*0.9492*	**0.9453**	0.7148
SLP (0.02)	0.7187	0.2656	**0.8789**	*0.8867*	**0.8427**	0.8792	0.6875	0.4335
GS (0.01)	0.6211	*0.8007*	**0.6836**	0.7070	0.8125	**0.7774**	0.5976	0.3828
SPLN (0.01)	0.7968	0.8359	*0.9883*	**0.8789**	**0.9493**	*0.9532*	0.8242	0.7929
SPLN (0.02)	**0.8086**	0.7109	0.7695	*0.9688*	**0.8906**	*0.9179*	0.7187	0.5156
CROP (10%)	0.5898	0.5625	*0.9102*	**0.8829**	0.5937	0.7539	**0.6703**	0.7820
CROP (20%)	0.3945	0.4726	*0.8516*	**0.7773**	0.7662	**0.6445**	0.5585	0.625
SCL (0.5)	0.9175	0.8086	0.9766	**0.9648**	0.9648	**0.9532**	0.8554	0.7382
SCL (0.9)	0.9846	**0.9726**	0.9414	0.9688	0.8125	**0.8789**	0.9023	0.8398
SCL (1.5)	0.9218	0.9375	*0.9844*	**0.9688**	**0.8438**	0.8477	0.8437	0.7734
JPEG (40)	**0.4570**	*0.6210*	0.4140	0.3398	**0.2734**	*0.6289*	0.2539	0.1718
JPEG (50)	0.5703	**0.6407**	*0.7109*	0.6406	0.4609	*0.6640*	**0.4882**	0.0195
JPEG (60)	0.5625	**0.6328**	*0.7304*	0.5234	**0.6289**	*0.7109*	−0.1679	0.3164
RT (0.1)	0.8046	0.8125	*0.9023*	**0.8828**	*0.7031*	**0.6406**	0.4336	0.5312

Table 9.2 NC value of extracted watermark for Peppers and House with PCA and without PCA

Image attacks	Peppers				House			
	With PCA		Without PCA		With PCA		Without PCA	
	Bagging	RS-KNN	Bagging	RS-KNN	Bagging	RS-KNN	Bagging	RS-KNN
SLP (0.01)	0.7226	**0.7656**	0.8476	0.6992	0.9375	0.5273	0.7617	**0.9062**
SLP (0.02)	0.5	0.6289	0.8710	0.6289	0.8242	0.8008	0.8554	0.8554
GS (0.01)	0.75	**0.6289**	0.5703	0.5976	**0.7734**	0.5742	0.7031	0.8007
SPLN (0.01)	0.8242	0.8086	**0.9140**	0.9258	0.6289	0.5352	**0.9062**	0.9101
SPLN (0.02)	0.6836	0.7349	0.8984	**0.8398**	0.7422	0.9231	**0.8828**	0.9179
CROP (10%)	0.5899	0.5625	0.9023	**0.8320**	0.5586	0.9067	**0.8710**	0.8984
CROP (20%)	0.3945	0.4726	0.8204	**0.7890**	0.6367	0.8712	**0.8164**	0.7578
SCL (0.5)	0.7031	0.7969	0.9179	0.9179	0.9648	0.5742	0.9414	**0.9219**
SCL (0.9)	0.7851	0.8906	**0.8906**	0.8945	0.9649	0.9258	0.9140	**0.9609**
SCL (1.5)	0.7422	0.7851	**0.8984**	0.8945	0.8867	0.8125	**0.9375**	0.9609
JPEG (40)	0.2460	0.4648	**0.4375**	0.1640	−0.1992	0.5234	**0.2421**	0.4765
JPEG (50)	**0.5273**	0.6210	0.4453	0.2890	0.6914	**0.6032**	0.7656	0.5546
JPEG (60)	0.3945	0.6484	**0.6406**	0.6250	0.8008	**0.5032**	0.7773	0.4531
RT (0.1)	0.7031	0.6133	**0.8242**	0.8672	0.7890	0.8007	**0.8867**	0.9101

Table 9.3 NC value of extracted watermark for Car and Jetplane with PCA and without PCA

Image attacks	Car				Jetplane			
	With PCA		Without PCA		With PCA		Without PCA	
	Bagging	RS-KNN	Bagging	RS-KNN	Bagging	RS-KNN	Bagging	RS-KNN
SLP (0.01)	0.6171	0.6054	**0.8710**	0.9063	0.3085	0.5898	0.9648	**0.7969**
SLP (0.02)	0.1875	0.2187	0.8281	**0.7539**	0.1484	0.4648	**0.7304**	0.7382
GS (0.01)	0.6210	0.6132	**0.8046**	0.8125	0.0664	0.4492	0.7929	**0.7304**
SPLN (0.01)	**0.8203**	0.1210	0.7695	0.8750	0.3320	0.7421	**0.8671**	0.9492
SPLN (0.02)	**0.6975**	0.4727	0.4882	0.8086	0.3984	0.6210	**0.5742**	0.6132
CROP (10%)	0.4062	0.4102	**0.6835**	0.7460	0.4531	0.6054	0.8359	**0.8320**
CROP (20%)	0.3516	0.4375	**0.6757**	0.7187	0.5273	0.5156	**0.7929**	0.8047
SCL (0.5)	0.6367	0.7696	**0.9140**	0.9258	0.5078	0.7929	0.9140	0.9140
SCL (0.9)	0.7539	0.5586	**0.7929**	0.9179	0.4882	0.8046	**0.7656**	0.8710
SCL (1.5)	0.6640	0.6796	**0.8828**	0.9257	0.5743	0.4882	0.9140	0.9140
JPEG (40)	−0.05	**0.3007**	0.4559	0.1796	**0.2031**	0.3453	0.1875	0.1992
JPEG (50)	0.5195	0.4179	0.5903	0.5820	**0.3320**	0.4453	0.2421	0.4921
JPEG (60)	0.5469	**0.4922**	0.6210	0.4765	0.5532	**0.5423**	0.3085	0.5234
RT (0.1)	0.3750	−0.3125	**0.6719**	0.6992	0.5390	0.1679	0.6992	**0.5468**

Table 9.4 NC value of extracted watermark for Lake and Zelda with PCA and without PCA

Image attacks	Lake				Zelda			
	With PCA		Without PCA		With PCA		Without PCA	
	Bagging	RS-KNN	Bagging	RS-KNN	Bagging	RS-KNN	Bagging	RS-KNN
SLP (0.01)	0.8710	**0.9023**	0.9218	0.8671	0.6836	0.7070	0.9375	**0.9140**
SLP (0.02)	0.8437	0.7617	0.9140	**0.7890**	0.5547	0.3125	0.7578	**0.7460**
GS (0.01)	0.8594	0.7734	0.8320	**0.8359**	0.6992	0.2460	0.7968	**0.5117**
SPLN (0.01)	0.8203	**0.9179**	0.9531	0.9170	0.6015	0.5469	**0.6289**	0.9804
SPLN (0.02)	0.9062	**0.8632**	0.9297	0.8164	0.6250	0.8320	**0.7851**	0.9336
CROP (10%)	0.6015	0.6562	**0.8594**	0.8903	0.7188	0.4297	**0.7929**	0.8242
CROP (20%)	0.5390	0.5234	0.7968	**0.7266**	0.6232	0.5937	0.7460	**0.7148**
SCL (0.5)	0.9101	0.8985	0.9531	**0.9101**	0.6953	0.5312	**0.8359**	0.9492
SCL (0.9)	0.9062	**0.9375**	0.9296	0.9258	**0.6758**	0.6719	0.6093	0.9453
SCL (1.5)	0.9375	**0.9218**	0.9062	0.9012	**0.7304**	0.7031	0.6835	0.9570
JPEG (40)	0.4335	0.0820	0.5273	**0.4882**	−0.1054	0.4560	**0.1953**	0.3750
JPEG (50)	0.5507	0.6406	**0.6171**	0.6367	0.2890	0.6456	0.6367	0.6367
JPEG (60)	0.4492	0.4765	**0.6601**	0.7070	0.6250	**0.6712**	0.7109	0.6610
RT (0.1)	**0.7734**	0.6132	0.6992	0.7843	0.7539	0.3437	**0.8046**	0.8867

and the RS-KNN model is 0.9883 for Lena without reducing the features and 0.9804 for the Zelda image without reducing the features. Likewise, the best NC value for the SPLN (0.02) attack for bagging and the RS-KNN model is 0.9297 for Lake and 0.9688 for the Lena image without feature reduction. The above results shows that it is not certain that with feature reduction only good results in terms of NC can be obtained, but in some case, without reducing the feature good results can be obtained.

9.4.4 Comparative study

The proposed ensemble model is compared with similar watermarking methods in terms of NC value and shown using Table 9.3, and bold value signifies that proposed model is outperforming other watermarking scheme. The sign of X shows the missing data.

Table 9.5 shows the comparison of performance against various image attacks using NC for image Lena, Peppers, and Mandril with Ernawan et al. [21] and Islam et al. [8]. The table clearly shows that proposed ensemble model performs well against SLP (0.01), SPLN (0.01), and SCL (0.5) attacks. One can notice that for JPEG attacks model is not performing good because the JPEG compression affect the relationship between pixel of watermarked image more then the other image attack. Figures 9.6 and 9.7

Table 9.5 Comparison of performance against various image attacks between Ernawan et al. (2021), Islam et al. (2018) and proposed ensemble model

Image attacks	Lena				Peppers			Mandril		
	Ernawan et al. [21]	Islam et al. [8]	Proposed model		Islam et al. [8]	Proposed model		Islam et al. [8]	Proposed model	
			Bagging	RS-KNN		Bagging	RS-KNN		Bagging	RS-KNN
SLP (0.01)	0.905	0.731	**0.9150**	**0.9688**	0.713	**0.8476**	**0.7656**	0.826	**0.9453**	**0.9492**
SLP (0.02)	0.850	X	**0.8789**	**0.8867**	X	0.8710	0.6289	X	0.8427	0.8792
SPLN (0.01)	0.811	0.738	**0.9883**	**0.8789**	0.775	**0.9140**	**0.9258**	0.779	**0.9493**	**0.9532**
SPLN (0.02)	0.976	X	0.8086	0.9688	X	0.8984	0.8398	X	0.8906	0.9179
CROP (10%)	X	0.917	**0.9172**	0.8829	0.907	0.9023	0.8320	0.831	0.6703	0.7820
CROP (20%)	X	0.937	0.8516	0.7773	0.941	0.8204	0.7890	0.756	**0.7662**	0.6445
SCL (0.5)	X	0.647	**0.9766**	**0.9648**	0.623	**0.9179**	0.9179	0.469	**0.9648**	**0.9532**

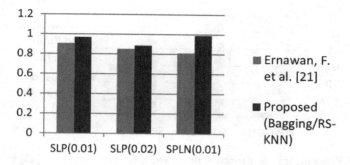

Figure 9.6 Comparison of proposed model with Ernawan, F. et al. [21] in terms of NC value.

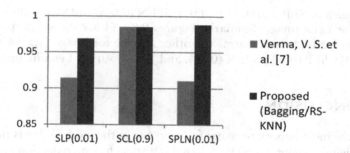

Figure 9.7 Comparison of proposed model with Verma, V. S. et al. [7] in terms of NC value.

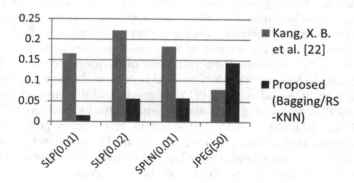

Figure 9.8 Performance comparison with Kang, X. B. et al. [22] in terms of BER.

show the performance comparison in terms of NC value, whereas Figures 9.8 and 9.9 show the comparison in terms of BER value.

Figures 9.6 and 9.7 clearly show that the proposed color image watermarking scheme outperforms the other similar existing method for image

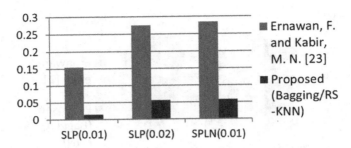

Figure 9.9 Performance comparison with Ernawan, F. and Kabir, M. N. [23] in terms of BER.

attacks such as SLP (0.01), SLP (0.02), SPLN (0.01), and SCL (0.9) in terms of NC for Lena image. Similarly, Figures 9.8 and 9.9 show that proposed ensemble method outperforms the other scheme for image attacks such as SLP (0.01), SLP (0.02), SPLN (0.01), and JPEG (50) for Lena image.

9.5 CONCLUSION

One of the most important issues for everyone in the modern day is the security of digital content. Using PCA-based statistical feature reduction and without feature reduction, an ensemble machine learning-based blind color image watermarking method has been suggested, which usages the IWT, ensemble-based machine learning model for watermark extraction. It is noticed that for some image attacks feature reduction based approach is showing good results and for some attacks without reducing feature performs well. Keys used at various level increases the security of the proposed system, and reducing the features using PCA improves the performance of the proposed system. Results for both BAGGING and RS-KNN method have been shown using the tables for both with PCA and without PCA approach, and it is noticed that both ML method is performing well against image attacks, such as SLP(0.01), SPLN(0.01), CROP(20%), and SCL(0.5) attacks. However, the proposed model could perform better against JPEG and RT attacks. This could be because these attacks affect the pixel relations more badly than any other image attacks. The same idea can be applied to the video and grayscale images.

REFERENCES

1. Hadipour, A., & Afifi, R. (2020). Advantages and disadvantages of using cryptography in Steganography. 17th International ISC Conference on Information Security and Cryptology (ISCISC), 88–94. DOI: 10.1109/ ISCISC51277.2020.9261921

2. Qin, C., Ji, P., Chang, C. C., Dong, J., & Sun, X. (2018). Non-uniform watermark sharing based on optimal iterative BTC for image tempering recovery. IEEE Multimedia, 25(3), 36–48.

3. Kumar, S., Singh B. K., & Yadav, M. (2020). A recent survey on multimedia and database watermarking. Multimedia Tools and Applications (2020) 79, 20149–20197.

4. Agarwal, N., Singh, A. K., & Singh, P. K. (2019). Survey of robust and imperceptible watermarking. *Multimedia Tools and Applications*, 78, 8603–8633.

5. Jaiswal, S., & Pandey, M. K. (2021). A Review on Image Segmentation. Conference Proceeding, Rising Threats in Expert Applications and Solutions, Springer, 233–240.

6. Fu, Y. G., & Shen, R. M. (2007). Color image watermarking scheme based on linear discriminate analysis. Computer Standard and Interface, Science Direct, 30, 115–120. DOI:10.1016/j.csi.2007.08.013

7. Verma, V.S., Jha, R.K., & Ojha, A. (2015). Digital watermark extraction using support vector machine with principal component analysis based feature reduction. Journal of Visual Communication and Image Representation, 31, 75–85.

8. Islam, M., & Laskar, R. H. (2018). Geometric distortion correction based robust watermarking scheme in LWT-SVD domain with digital watermark extraction using SVM. Multimedia Tools Application, 77(11), 14407–14434. https://doi.org/10.1007/s11042-017-5035-9

9. Chang, T. J., Pan, I. H., Huang, P. S., & Hu, C. H. (2018). A robust DCT-2DLDA watermark for color images. Multimedia Tools and Applications. https://doi.org/10.1007/s11042-018-6505-4

10. Sharma, S., Sharma, H., Sharma, J. B., & Poonia, R. C. (2020). A secure and robust color image watermarking using nature inspired intelligence. Neural Computing and Application. https://doi.org/10.1007/s00521-020-05634-8

11. Anand, A., & Singh, A. K. (2020). An improved DWT-SVD domain watermarking for medical information security. Computer Communications, 152, 72–80. https://doi.org/10.1016/j.comcom.2020.01.038

12. Sinhal, R., Jain, D. K., & Ansari, I. A. (2021). Machine learning based blind color image watermarking scheme for copyright protection. Patter Recognition Letter, 145, 171–177.

13. Jaiswal, S., & Pandey, M. K. (2022). Robust digital image watermarking using LWT and random-subspace-1DLDA with PCA based statistical feature reduction. 2022 Second International Conference on Computer Science, Engineering and Applications (ICCSEA), 1–6.

14. Barlaskar, S. A., Singh, S. V., Monsley, A., & Laskar, R. H. (2022). Genetic algorithm based optimized watermarking technique using hybrid DCNN-SVR and statistical approach for watermark extraction. Multimedia Tools and Applications. https://doi.org/10.1007/s11042-021-11798.9

15. Bingham, G. (2017). Random Subspace Two-Dimensional LDA for Face Recognition. arXiv:1711.00575v1

16. Sweldens, W. (1996). The lifting scheme: A custom-design construction of biorthogonal wavelets. Applied and Computational Harmonic Analysis, 3, 186–200.

17. Zhang, Y., Cao, G., Wang, B., & Li, X. (2019). A novel ensemble method for k-nearest neighbor. Pattern Recognition, 85, 13–25, https://doi.org/10.1016/j.patcog.2018.08.003

18. Ho, T. K. (1998). Nearest neighbors in random subspaces, Bell Laboratories, Lucent Technologies 700 Mountain Avenue. 2C-425, Murray Hill, NJ 07974, USA.
19. Jolliffe, Principal Component Analysis. Springer-Verlag, 1986.
20. http://www.imageprocessingplace.com/root_files_V3/image_databases.htm (Accessed 10 Feb 2022).
21. Ernawan, F., Ariatmanto, D., & Firdaus, A. (2021). An improved image watermarking by modifying selected DWT-DCT coefficients. IEEE Access, 9, 45474–45485.
22. Kang, X. B., Zhao, F., Lin, G-F., & Chen, Y. J. (2018). A novel hybrid of DCT and SVD in DWT domain for robust and invisible blind image watermarking with optimal embedding strength. Multimedia Tools and Application, 77(11), 13197–13224.
23. Ernawan, F., & Kabir, M. N. (2018). A robust image watermarking technique with an optimal DCT-psycho-visual threshold. IEEE Access, 6, 20464–20480.

Index

Note: **Bold** page numbers refer to tables; *italic* page numbers refer to figures.

abuse 36
Agenzia Nazionale Stampa Associata
    (ANSA) 27
ALBERT 53
AR *see* autoregressive model (AR)
ARIMA *see* Autoregressive Integrated
    Moving Average (ARIMA)
ARMA *see* autoregressive moving
    average models (ARMA)
artificial bee colony (ABC)
    optimization 115
artificial intelligence (AI)
    algorithmic disinformation
        detection 6
    correct and downplay false
        content 10
    deep-learning algorithms 103–104
    detect and get rid of false
        information 6
    digital and media literacy 11–12
    diplomacy 11
    double-edged sword 12
    fake news (*see* fake news)
    fraudulent bot accounts 105
    higher accountability and
        openness 10
    natural language processing
        strategies 102–103
    shortcomings 6–7
    social media regulations 11
    socio-technological and
        multidisciplinary approach 9
    technological countermeasures 10
    techplomacy 11

audio abuse detection 39, 42
aural abuse 38
authenticity 60, 64
Autoregressive Integrated Moving
    Average (ARIMA) 87
autoregressive model (AR) 87
autoregressive moving average models
    (ARMA) 87

bagging classification method
    117, 125
BCT *see* blockchain technology (BCT)
Bidirectional Encoder Representations
    from Transformers (BERT)
    51–52, *52*
Bi-LSTM model 55
binary classification method 118
binary watermark 115
Bitcoin transactions 64
bit error rate (BER) 114, 122
blind grayscale image
    watermarking 116
blockchain technology (BCT)
    7–8, 9, 21
    application 12, 27–28, *28*
    businesses and finance 24
    cost of implementations 28
    cutting-edge technology 14
    education 25
    fake news (*see* fake news)
    features 9
    healthcare 25
    literature review 21–24, *22–24*
    news credibility 8

blockchain technology (*cont.*)
    noninteractive zero-knowledge
        proof 62, *62*
    organisational challenges 29
    provenance check 12–14
    regulatory challenges 29–30
    scalability challenges 29
    solution with 14–15
    supply chain and logistics 25
    traceability 9
bot-labeling techniques 105

classical time series methods 87–88
conditional probability 71
convolutional neural networks
    (CNNs) 50
co-occurrence analysis 22–23, *24*
cryptography 65, 114
cutting-edge technology 14
cyber bullying, statistics 35, *36*
cyber security 59, 60

data preprocessing 51
DCT-2DLDA-based blind
    watermarking scheme 115
decision trees (DR) 72, *78*
deep learning techniques 88–89
    artificial intelligence 103–104
    audio abuse detection 42
    data preprocessing 51
    multimodal learning strategy 39
    online abuse and hate analysis
        39, **40–41**
    standard research methodology
        42, *42*
    transformer-based models 51–55
deep neural networks 104
digital image watermarking 113
digital literacy 2, 11–12
digital media ecology 3–4
disinformation 3, 99
DistilBERT 52, *53*
distributed ledger approach 25
domain-wise representation,
    of documents 22, *23*

ensemble-based watermarking 116
ensemble model 127, **128**, *129*,
    129–130, *130*
exploratory data analysis (EDA) 73, *75*

Facebook 68
Factcheck 68

fact-checking organizations 68
facticity 3
fake news 2
    artificial intelligence 5–7
    blockchain technology 7–9
    content moderation verify 26
    effects of 101
    and growing issues 3–4
    identification 68–81
    internet 20
    in journalism 4–5
    most frequent words 77, *80*
    natural language processing
        strategies 102–103
    prediction 76, *76*
    prevalence of 16
    process of curbing 105–107
    social media 20, 21, 27
    source of origin verify 26
    by tracking 26–27
    types 20
Fiat–Shamir heuristic 61
forecasting 85
Fourth Industrial Revolution (IR4.0) 16

gatekeeping 70
genesis block 24
GPT-3 104

hate speech 9, 38, 50
Holt Winter's Exponential Smoothing
    (HWES) 88

image watermarking 113–114
    proposed color scheme 118–122
imperceptibility 114, 123, *124*
integer wavelet transform (IWT)
    114, 117
interactive zero-knowledge proof 61
internet surfers 14
invisible watermark 114

journalism
    and fake news 4–5
    implications 4
    news values in 101

lifting wavelet transform (LWT)
    see integer wavelet
    transform (IWT)
logistic regression (LR) 72–73, *78*
Long Short-Term Memory (LSTM)
    89, *91*

machine learning (ML)
  data preparation 73–75, *74*, *75*
  image watermarking 114
  implement 68
  inter-model comparison 81, *81*
  intra-model comparison 80, *81*
  model evaluation 76, **76**
  TF–IDF 75
MAE *see* mean absolute error (MAE)
MAPE *see* mean absolute percentage
      error (MAPE)
McAfee 35, *36*
mean absolute error (MAE) 90
mean absolute percentage error
      (MAPE) 89, *91*
mean squared error (MSE) 90, 122
Mel-frequency cepstral coefficients
      (MFCCs) 42–43
MetaFact 6, 105
MSE *see* mean squared error (MSE)
multimedia datasets 39

Naive Bayes (NB) 71, 77
natural language processing (NLP)
      strategies 102–103
news values
  defined 2
  implications on 4
  in journalism 101
non-fungible token (NFT) artwork 8
noninteractive zero-knowledge proof
      62, *62*

online abuse 38
online news ecosystem 2
OpenAI 104
opinion mining *see* sentiment analysis

passive aggressive algorithm (PAA)
      73, *79*
pattern recognition 105
peak signal-to-noise ratio (PSNR)
      114, 122
Pew Research Center 36
PolitiFact 68
principal component analysis (PCA) 117
Prophet 88–89, *90*

random forest (RF) 72, 77
Random subspace-KNN
      (RS-KNN) 117
real news, most frequent words
      77, *79*, *80*

real-time stock data 86
recurrent neural network (RNN)
      model 53–54, *54*
  accuracy and loss 55, **55**, *56*
  preprocessing 51
RMSE *see* root mean squared
      error (RMSE)
RoBERTa 52–53
robustness 114, 125–126,
      125–127, 127
root mean squared error (RMSE) 90

Seasonal Autoregressive Integrated
      Moving Average
      (SARIMA) 87
semi-fragile watermarking system 114
sentiment analysis 49
SES *see* Simple Exponential
      Smoothing (SES)
ShareChat 42
"shielded" option 63
sigmoid feature *see* logistic
      regression (LR)
Simple Exponential Smoothing
      (SES) 88
singular value decomposition
      (SVD) 115
Snopes 68
social media
  businesses 105
  effects 97
  emergence of 68
  engagement and connectivity 96
  outlets 96, 98–101
  platforms 20, 21
  usage 96
  users 21
S-shaped regression model 72–73
steganography 114
stemming 74–75
stock price data 86
stop word removal 74
support vector machine (SVM) 72

techplomacy 11
tensor processing units (TPUs) 54
term frequency (TF)–inverse dense
      frequency (IDF) technique 75
text mining technologies 49
time series forecasting models 85
  classical time series methods
      87–88
  data collection and preprocessing 86

time series forecasting models (*cont.*)
   deep learning–based methods
      88–89
   training and performance
      evaluation 89
   types 87
tokenization 74
toxicity analysis 49–57
transfer learning 39
transformer-based models
   ALBERT 53
   BERT 51–52, *52*
   DistilBERT 52, *53*
   preprocessing 51
   RoBERTa 52–53
Twitter 42, 68

VGG16 43
video editing 104

watermark embedding process
   118–120, *120*
watermark extraction process
   120–122, *121*
WhatsApp 2

Zcash coin 63
zero knowledge proof (ZKP) 60–61
   authentication systems 65
   bibliometrics analyses 63
   interactive 61
   noninteractive 62, *62*
   virtuous behavior 65
   Zcash coin 63
   zk-SNARKs 64
   zk-STARKs 64–65

Printed in the United States
by Baker & Taylor Publisher Services